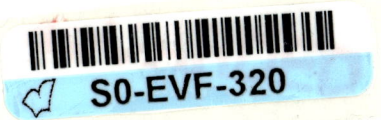

CROSSING THE SHADOW-LINE

Gustave Doré's illustration for Coleridge's *The Rime of the Ancient Mariner*.

CROSSING THE SHADOW-LINE

The Literature of Estrangement

MARTIN BOCK

Ohio State University Press
Columbus

Copyright © 1989 by the Ohio State University Press.
All rights reserved.

Library of Congress Cataloging-in-Publication Data

Bock, Martin, 1951–
    Crossing the shadow-line : the literature of estrangement /
Martin Bock.
        p. cm.
    Bibliography: p.
    Includes index.
    ISBN 0–8142–0471–6
    1. English fiction—20th century—History and criticism.
2. Alienation (Philosophy) in literature. 3. Orientation (Psychology)
in literature. 4. Senses and sensation in literature. 5. English
literature—19th century—History and criticism. 6. American
literature—History and criticism. I. Title.
PR888.A42C76 1989
820'.9'353—dc19   88–25075

The paper in this book meets the guidelines for permanence and durability
of the Committee on Production Guidelines for Book Longevity of the
Council on Library Resources.

Printed in the U.S.A.

ECC/USF LEARNING RESOURCES
8099 College Parkway, S.W.
P. O. Box 06210
Fort Myers, FL 33906-6210

For my mother and father

Contents

Acknowledgments		ix
Introduction: On Sensation, Knowledge, and Cultural Perception		1
Sensation and the Philosophy of Mind		
Disjoining the Cultural Episteme		
One	Coleridge and the Subversion of Archetypes	13
Two	Thomas De Quincey's Defect of the Eye	26
	Departure from the Wordsworthian Landscape	
	The Subversion of Archetypes	
	Mechanical Models of Mind	
Three	Poe and the French Symbolists: Disjoining the Cultural Episteme	45
	Baudelaire and the Theory of Correspondances	
	Poe and the Disjoining of Cultural Value	
	Rimbaud's Dérèglement de Tous les Sens	
Four	The Nocturnal Visions of Joyce and Barnes	65
	Joyce, Epiphany, and the Association of Sensibility	
	Barnes's Nightwood and the "Evacuation" of Custom	
Five	Joseph Conrad and the Shadow-Line of Disorientation	85
	Sensation, Knowledge, Image	
	The Disorienting Voyage	
Six	Malcolm Lowry's Manichean Episteme: The Paradise of Despair	115
	The Linguistic Basis of Lowry's Episteme	

The Imagery of Disorientation: Vertiginous
and Entropic Extremes
Under the Volcano: *The Structure of
Disorientation*

Conclusion: Eccentricity and the Horizon of
Expectations   140

Notes   147

Works Cited   155

Index   165

Acknowledgments

I would first like to thank Phil Herring for his unerring, sound advice throughout the course of my work on this project. J. Kastely and Mike Clark I thank for their long-distance encouragement. I am grateful to the University of Hawaii for a grant during the initial stages of research and to the University of Minnesota for a timely Faculty Summer Research Fellowship. Anne Yandle and her staff at the University of British Columbia Special Collections were most helpful during my research of Malcolm Lowry's papers. Milan Kovacovic provided valuable suggestions on the translations of Baudelaire and Rimbaud. Robert Lance Snyder, Henry S. Sussman, and David Leon Higdon offered generous advice and support of my work. Finally, I am indebted to Carol Bock, my wife and colleague, for her thorough and intelligent criticism of virtually every page of this book.

Introduction:
On Sensation, Knowledge, and Cultural Perception

Is not the truth the truth?
—Falstaff, *King Henry IV*, I

Thus men, extending their inquiries beyond their capacities, and letting their thoughts wander into those depths where they can find no sure footing, it is no wonder that they raise questions and multiply disputes, which, never coming to any clear resolution, are proper only to increase their doubts, and to confirm them at last in perfect scepticism.
—John Locke, *An Essay Concerning Human Understanding*

Sensation and the Philosophy of Mind

The captain in Conrad's *The Shadow-Line* begins his narration by musing on the course of our human lives. Early in life, he reflects, "One closes behind one the little gate of mere boyishness—and enters an enchanted garden." But after the "seduction" of the paths of youth, one inevitably comes to a shadow-line, the boundary between youth and experience: "One goes on," he continues. "And the time, too, goes on—till one perceives ahead a shadow-line warning one that the region of early youth, too, must be left behind" (17:3). As we read this, our cultural associations with innocence and experience are immediately triggered. Whether or not we are practicing Christians, most of us think of the Garden of Eden when the narrator mentions an "enchanted garden"; we think of Adam and Eve and of transgression when he mentions seduction and warning; and we think of expulsion and exile when we imagine crossing the shadow-line, leaving behind the region of early youth. We have these thoughts in part because we are trained readers, poised for the imaginative leap, but also because Conrad is a practiced artist who knows how we, as members of a predominantly Christian culture, will respond to his seemingly casual allusions.

This study explores the region beyond the shadow-line but not in the literal sense that Conrad suggests. Rather, *Crossing the Shadow-Line* looks at the link between perception and exile implied in the opening paragraphs of Conrad's novella. In much of Conrad's work, the shadow-line is a demarcation between the familiar and the unfamiliar, the time and place at which one becomes estranged from one's culture and the body of knowledge available or useful in that culture. The chapters that follow examine writers from the romantic through the modern periods who are fascinated with characters, narrators, or speakers who become estranged from their cultures. While recognizing the authority structures and mythos of the dominant Christian culture, these figures perceive and act in a manner that significantly departs from what is culturally acceptable, and thus they are heretical. Similarly, the authors themselves, whether or not they embrace or reject Christian values, are heretical in that they inadvertently or willfully subvert the cultural episteme, that body of knowledge associated with cultural attitudes toward sensation, language, imagination, symbolism and mythical archetypes.

I use the notion of cultural episteme in its broad and literal sense as an assumed, "certain knowledge" of the world that each individual, however variously, possesses—that is, the conventional codes of reality instilled in us by our society, our culture or, more broadly, our civilization. It is not my intent to explore the cultural episteme in the way Foucault has by defining a taxonomy or "archeology" of the classical episteme in *The Order of Things*,[1] but I shall briefly survey some of the philosophic assumptions of our culture, particularly with respect to concepts of sensation; for the philosophic discourse on sensation provides the adherents of this culture with an understanding of the way we see and provides the writers in the heretical tradition with the cultural values to subvert.

One basic assumption that determines what our civilization

considers as knowable is the truism that our bodies are, in some basic way, inferior to our minds. This premise is metaphorically presented in what is probably the most widely known philosophic analogy in the Western tradition, Plato's "Allegory of the Cave," at the beginning of Book 7 of the *Republic*. Plato's famous visual metaphor of sense perception suggests that bodily senses are faculties which enslave us and point us toward false representations of reality, mere shadows of higher reality. The mark of Plato's idealist allegory and his overt derogation of the senses can be easily traced in the major philosophic thinkers who follow him. Like his predecessor, Aristotle prefaces his discourse on the human mind with the assertion that there are two orders of the apprehension of knowledge, one through the mind and another through the senses. He categorically states, in *De Anima*, that the apprehension of the soul is superior to that of the senses:

> We regard knowledge as a good and a precious thing, but we esteem one sort of knowledge more highly than another either because of the acumen required for its discovery, or because it is concerned with better and more admirable objects: for both these reasons we should rightly assign the investigation of the soul to the first rank. (Aristotle 1–2)

In his discourse on human psychology, Aristotle finds that the soul "apparently neither acts nor is acted upon independently of the body" and yet, in its indivisibility from the body, possesses the exclusive properties of thought and imagination (6). The discourse asserts that while body and soul are inseparable, the soul, as an entity which "realizes an idea," is distinct from the body which houses it. Intellection is thus deemed superior to sensation, and Aristotle metaphorically compares the various perceptions of body and soul:

> If the eye were an animal, vision would be its soul, i.e. vision is the notional essence of the eye. . . . As vision and pupil on the one hand constitute the eye, so soul and body in the other case constitute the living animal. (46)

Clearly, as St. Thomas Aquinas would later recognize (1:806), Aristotle's discourse assumes a closer connection between the senses and the intellect than does Plato's idealism. And yet Aristotle's rationalist philosophy nonetheless continues the model of mind which relegates the human senses to a rudimentary, preliminary mode of understanding that reveals only lesser truths about the nature of reality.

The Aristotelian model of mind that grows out of the discourses of *De Anima* and *De Sensu* posits three kinds of knowledge apprehended by the soul: sense-perception, reflective thought, and imaginative conception (106–7). Offering a kind of trinity of perceptual modes, the Aristotelian model quite naturally appealed to important Christian philosophers such as St. Augustine and St. Thomas Aquinas, whose models of mind served our culture until the late seventeenth century. Like Aristotle, Augustine envisions three kinds of metaphysical reality—body, human soul, and creator—and again suggests that "the conscious soul (*animus*) is better than the body . . . [which is] always less than the soul itself" (45–46). Augustine also envisioned three levels of perception that correspond to these levels of reality: the corporeal senses, the spirit, and, finally, "imageless" intellectual vision. These three levels of knowing form a distinct hierarchy, "so that reason may ascend from the lower to the higher" (95–96). The lower form, which comes through the bodily senses, does not attain to true knowledge which comes through what Augustine calls the interior sense which is akin to reason. Intellectual vision is, of course, the highest form of knowledge and remote from lowly sensation. Following Augustine's lead, St. Thomas, in the *Summa Theologica*, distinguishes exterior from interior senses (Aquinas 1:738–44) and concludes "the judgment of the intellect is higher than the senses" (1:810). Using St. Augustine as an authority, St. Thomas argues that "we cannot expect to learn the truth from the senses. . . . Intellectual knowledge apprehends the truth" (2:805). Augustinian and Thomistic theory, which gracefully adapt the secular model of Aristotle to religious purposes, retain the basic division between body and soul.

There is, of course, a school of materialist philosophy whose theories of sensation differ from those of the idealist tradition outlined above. But these thinkers did not achieve intellectual respectability until the time of Descartes, whose epistemology largely upheld the idealist division between mind and body but emphasized the importance of understanding the physical causes of sensation and perception.[2] It was not until the eighteenth century, a period that spawned controversy regarding all questions of epistemology, that we see a major shift in the cultural attitude toward sensation. In a number of ways, the English empiricists offer the most interesting departure from the Aristotelian tradition, even though as a group they have some similarities with their rationalist and theological predecessors.[3]

If Locke may be taken as the seminal thinker of this group, which includes Berkeley and Hume, we see that the first empiricist document, *An Essay Concerning Human Understanding*, directly descends from the tradition outlined above. Locke's pronouncements—*"All ideas come from sensation or reflection"* and "perception . . . might properly enough be called 'internal sense' " (Ayer 43)—are pronouncements that might have been made by his predecessors. What separates Locke from idealist or rationalist thinkers are those philosophic assumptions that we most commonly associate with empiricism, that humans are not born with any innate understanding in the soul—the mind is a tabula rasa—and that the vast store of ideas in the human mind comes from our own experience:

> Our observation, employed either about external sensible objects, or about the internal operations of our minds, perceived and reflected on by ourselves, is that which supplies our understanding with all the materials of thinking. (Ayer 43)

During the late seventeenth century, Locke rearranged the cultural hierarchy of modes of understanding. In his view, sensation is no longer a crude, preliminary mode of understanding; it is the "great source of most of the ideas we have" (Ayer 43). This primary role of sensation in the empiricist model of mind challenges the traditional valuations of body and soul and suggests that the soul or intellect is not necessarily the superior mode for understanding reality. Since much of the cultural, Christian concept of human understanding is based on the earlier idealist philosophy, this new emphasis on the primacy of sensation is essentially a heretical departure from the way our culture had traditionally described our relation to the physical world. A seemingly minor shift in the way Locke describes the relation of sensation and knowledge thus signified a major shift in the cultural episteme.

Locke's successors challenged and furthered his ideas. In *A Treatise Concerning the Principles of Human Knowledge,* Berkeley suggests that "ideas of sense are more strong, lively, and *distinct* than those of the imagination" (Ayer 189), and in *A Treatise Concerning Human Nature,* Hume concurs:

> Those perceptions which enter with most force and violence, we may name *impressions;* and, under this name, I comprehend all our sensations, passions, and emotions, as they make their first appearance in the soul. By *ideas,* I mean the faint images of these in thinking and reasoning; such as, for instance, are all the perceptions excited by the present discourse. (Ayer 298)

This new emphasis on sensation and feeling in philosophy of mind significantly influenced the major literary figures of the next century. The degree to which the first generation of English romantics embraced or rejected the ideas of the empiricists is still a matter of scholarly discussion and debate.[4] We can say with confidence, however, that the empiricist tendency to validate individual sensation and feeling as a way of knowing the world is a philosophic premise congenial to the romantic sensibility as it developed in the late eighteenth century.

In particular, Wordsworth and Coleridge shared aesthetic preoccupations that grew out of the central philosophic problems of the eighteenth century. Reformulating the philosophic questions in artistic terms, the first generation of romantics implied that what is true about the acquisition of knowledge may also be true about the poetic imagination. While the poets naturally give more credence than do the philosophers to the validity of the active imagination, both sets of thinkers recognized that vividness of sensation plays a primary role in the issue of representation, whether as part of an epistemological or artistic process. Accordingly, in his opening remarks to the second edition of *Lyrical Ballads*, Wordsworth suggests that poetry must reflect "the real language of men in a state of vivid sensation" (16). Later, Coleridge extends this notion about artistic representation in the *Biographia Literaria* (Zall 160n):

> Images however beautiful, though faithfully copied from nature, and as accurately represented in words, do not of themselves characterize the poet. They become proofs of original genius only as far as they are modified by a predominant passion; or by associated thoughts or images awakened by that passion. (7, 2:23)

Coleridge's idea that the poet's signature of genius is the way his or her imagination modifies representations of nature marks a significant departure from the Aristotelian philosophy of mind and the *Poetics*, which defines a mimetic poesis.[5] This romantic literary epistemology, which theoreticians have labeled the "projective imagination" or "expressive theory of art,"[6] is individual-centered and validates the primacy of sensation *and* emotion in representing a poetic reality to the reader.

The subjectivity of Berkeley and the romantics was extended in the late nineteenth and early twentieth centuries. Sensationist thinkers such as Ernst Mach radically assert, like Berkeley, that "the world consists only of our sensation" (10). But unlike his predecessors, Mach, a mathematician and physicist, suggests antimetaphysical theories in which objective science describes the human experience of the phenomenal world:

> Bodies do not produce sensations, but complexes of sensations (complexes of elements) make up bodies. If, to the physicist, bodies appear the real, abiding existences, whilst sensations are regarded merely as their evanescent, transitory show, the physicist forgets, in the assumption of such a view, that all bodies are but thought-

symbols for complexes of sensations (complexes of elements). Here, too, the *elements* form the real, immediate, and ultimate foundation, which it is the task of physiological research to investigate. (22)

Mach's late-nineteenth-century study of physiological perception anticipated Wittgenstein and the Vienna Circle of logical positivists.[7] Also known as logical empiricists, this group of thinkers is typically regarded as an outgrowth of English empiricism, for they consider assertions about the objective, external world meaningless. Wittgenstein and his followers thus shift the study of perception from an epistemology of objects to a psychology of reality. In his *Blue Book* and *Brown Book*, a series of Cambridge University lecture notes, Wittgenstein discusses his ideas about sensation, language, and the relation between the two. He discusses the "locality of thinking" (16) and suggests a metaphorical model of mind in which our thoughts are compared to the shadow cast by a physical object, a model seemingly the obverse of Plato's (36). Later, in *Philosophical Investigations*, he systematically explores the privacy of sensations (246–48), the manner in which words represent sensation (243–44), and the relation between language and inner experience (256).

These philosophic developments are again reflected in the concerns of the leading literary figures of the late nineteenth and early twentieth centuries. Joseph Conrad, in many of his prefaces, stresses that the primary task of the artist is to put the reader in intense contact with what he called the "visible universe." Like Mach, Conrad views human sensation as indicative of experience and suggests that the task of the artist is to capture the sensation of the moment, "to show its vibration, its colour, its form; and through its movement, its form, its colour, reveal the substance of its truth" (*Prefaces* 52). For Conrad, sensation is substance or objective reality. Other modern writers, most notably Joyce, experiment with fictional forms which demonstrate the linguistic creation of reality, a notion consistent with Wittgenstein's philosophical tracts. Eugene Jolas, close friend and publisher of Joyce, suggests that Joyce led nothing less than the "Revolution of the Word" (29–31) by destroying our cultural sense of the relation between the phenomenal world, language, and the human mind. The modern philosophical interest in sensation, linked to the role language plays in the human creation of reality, is thus a clear antecedent of the nineteenth-century literary interest in the representation of sensation by the projective imagination. Both models of mind offer an epistemological process that departs from the cultural episteme of the Christian era.

Disjoining the Cultural Episteme

I have emphasized the role of sensation in the above survey of cultural perception because the authors discussed in the following chapters are writers who demonstrate or portray the deliberate derangement of sensation in a way that violates our idealist cultural episteme. Though cultural perception obviously entails more than a shared attitude toward sensation—and may include such cultural givens as language, images, symbols, or archetypes—the literary artist inevitably confronts the aesthetic choice of how to represent sensation in his or her work. In the case of nineteenth-century writers such as Coleridge, De Quincey, Poe, and the French symbolists, the interest in matters of epistemology not only centers on sensation, but that sensation is colored by more than the human imagination. Each of these artists, at some point in his career, came under the influence of artificial stimulants, either opium or alcohol, which induce sensate experiences that are radically different from those offered by everyday cultural reality. Many later modern writers, such as Conrad, Joyce, Barnes, and Lowry, were also influenced by their experiences with drugs or alcohol, although by the twentieth century it is likely that the sense disorientation that we see in their works is a mixture of personal experience and conventionalized imagery. In either case, the disorientation of the senses provided all of these writers with imagery and vocabulary that set them apart from more mainstream writers who embraced the cultural codes of perception.

Roland Barthes, in a discussion of writing and reading processes in his *The Pleasure of the Text*, distinguishes between writers who embrace the cultural episteme and those who reject it in his discussion of writing and reading processes. The text of pleasure, he argues, "contents, fills, grants euphoria; the text that comes from culture and does not break with it, is linked to a *comfortable* practice of reading." This, clearly, describes the writer who seeks to confirm our a priori values and sense of reality. The writer who abandons the cultural episteme, on the other hand, offers a "text of bliss"

> that imposes a state of loss, the text that discomforts (perhaps to the point of a certain boredom), unsettles the reader's historical, cultural, psychological assumptions, the consistency of his tastes, values, memories, brings to a crisis his relation with language. (14)

Such writers create discomfort or a sense of cultural estrangement in a number of ways. Typically, the writers in this study unsettle the reader's cultural assumptions through sensory derangement which is accompanied by analogous forms of linguistic or symbolic disorientation. If there is a hierarchy of such forms of disorientation, it might be compared to the forms of knowledge in the cultural episteme as follows:

ADHERENCE TO CULTURE	ESTRANGEMENT FROM CULTURE
Sensate Knowledge (Body)	Disorientation of Senses (Percepts)
Intellectual Knowledge (Soul)	Disorientation of Language (Thought)
	Disorientation of Images (Imagination)
Spiritual Knowledge (God)	Disorientation of Symbols (Signs)
	Disorientation of Archetypes (Myths)

The form of disorientation most important to this study, *disorientation of the senses,* is often based on drug-related experiences or conventions that grow out of that experience. Chief among these is simple hyperesthesia, or the supersensitivity of the senses. From a clinical standpoint, hyperesthesia is unusual tactile sensitivity; this medical sense may be extended to include other sensations that are exaggerated by the drug experience, including the "sense" of time and space.[8] Synesthesia, or the stimulation of one type of sensation by a different type of sensation, is a second form of disorientation, long discounted in the rationalist tradition.[9] Associated with the genuine synesthesia, literary synesthesia is a convention that suggests the transcendence of ordinary perception through imaginary vision. Finally, anesthesia, the cessation of sense stimuli and the opposite of hyperesthesia, also marks a departure from the realm of conventional perception.

Writers who are fascinated by such extraordinary sensations often create an analogous kind of *linguistic disorientation,* which can assume many forms. On the level of words, recent practitioners of the verbocentric text have experimented with neologisms and multilingual puns. On a stylistic level, they have used digression or prose that depends heavily on abstract associations. Structurally, writers in this tradition have sometimes used multiple texts which visually compete with each other for the reader's attention and disrupt the normal activity of reading. Finally, these writers have treated linguistic disorientation thematically by making communication between characters difficult or confusing or by creating language that resists interpretation.

A third form of disjoining cultural value is through *imagistic* or *symbolic disorientation.* When an author consciously desecrates a symbolic object or image, he or she effectively denigrates the cultural value attached to it. Likewise, if a traditional object is appropriated for personal use, the individuation of its value is an attack on cultural value. This iconoclasm is closely related to the fourth form of disorientation, *mythic* or *archetypal disorientation,* which occurs when an important mythic or archetypal pattern is subverted through parody, farce, or irony. The subversion of archetypes, which occurs when an author modifies an important moral, mythical, or religious story, generally occurs on a structural level, when the plot or occurrences of an archetypal pattern are violated in such a way as to challenge the cultural value implied by that pattern.

All of these forms of disorientation are means for disjoining the cultural episteme, for each instance of sensate, cognitive, or imaginative disorientation in a work of literature contributes to an estrangement from the value of that culture. The remaining chapters examine the literary tradition of disorientation, a tradition distinct from the Christian tradition of an archetypal circular journey. In this heretical tradition, estrangement from one's cultural landscape begins with a disorienting voyage and ends with the protagonist shedding cultural assumptions, accepting a new mode of perception, and refusing reintegration into the culture. To depict this subversion of cultural perception, major writers such as Coleridge, De Quincey, Poe, Baudelaire, Rimbaud, Conrad, Joyce, Barnes, and Lowry all adopt the imagistic and structural convention of sense disorientation, and in so doing they cross the shadow-line that marks the boundary of heretical space.

One
Coleridge and the Subversion of Archetypes

The poet in his lone yet genial hour
Gives to his eyes a magnifying power:
Or rather he emancipates his eyes
From the black shapeless accidents of size—
In unctuous cones of kindling coal,
Or smoke upwreathing from the pipe's trim bole,
  His gifted ken can see
  Phantoms of sublimity.
      —S. T. Coleridge, "Apologia Pro Vita Sua"

While the first generation of romantics shared an aesthetic or even epistemological interest in the issue of representation, their poetry shows divergent understandings of the relation between sensation and imagination. These differences make it difficult to think of them as a generation at all, for two separate literary traditions can be discerned within this group. When Coleridge, in 1817, distinguished his poetic endeavor from that of his collaborator in *Lyrical Ballads*, he identified two traditions that would dominate nonrealist Western literature for the next two centuries. These traditions, generally associated with the romantic and symbolist movements, have been assumed by historical scholars to reach full expression in consecutive historical periods, but in fact the romantic and symbolist impulses are evident in the works of Wordsworth and Coleridge respectively and are continued in individual writers through the modern period. In the *Biographia Literaria*, Coleridge alludes to these respective traditions in his discussion of the "Occasion of the Lyrical Ballads," where he consigns to Wordsworth the writing of poetry that exhibits "a faithful adherence to the truth of nature" and to himself poetry offering "the interest of novelty [given] by the modifying colours of imagination" (7, 2:5). Such a distinction on Coleridge's part indicates his sense of the clear differences between his own and Wordsworth's verse. More importantly, the two kinds of poetry that Coleridge identifies reveal different models of mind which, in turn, presuppose different epistemologies, one associated with the dominant Christian-romantic episteme and the other with a heretical symbolist episteme that subverts the mythos and archetypes of the dominant culture.

Romantic criticism of the last few decades, most notably that of Abrams and Frye, has identified the Christian mythos as the basis of Wordsworthian romanticism. Coleridge offered a similar assessment, acknowledging the essential Christian nature of Wordsworth's poetry in its *"faithful* adherence to the *truth"* of a natural world [emphasis added]. This mimetic poesis, in which the poet faithfully ratifies an innate sense of the truth of nature, suggests the cultural and religious orthodoxy of Wordsworth's work, for "nature" is a cultural denotation for the works of God. As a symbolist, Coleridge requires of himself a more individual and humanistic task, to create "novelty" and to modify through imagination what is normally perceived as the natural world. In creating a supernatural poetic landscape, Coleridge seeks "to transfer from our inward nature a human interest and a semblance of truth sufficient to procure for these shadows of imagination that willing suspension of disbelief for the moment, which constitutes poetic faith" (7, 2:6). Coleridge's poetic endeavors offer a kind of literary heresy by supplanting the culturally sanctioned Christian faith with a human poetic faith.[1] Similarly, his celebrated definition of the "Primary Imagination" depends on a religious analogy; Coleridge holds the Primary Imagination "to be the living Power and prime Agent of all human Perception, and as a repetition in the finite mind of the eternal act of creation in the infinite I AM" (7, 1:304). Like a God of creation, the supernatural poet crosses into a region of the shadowy imagination and produces a *semblance* of truth which the adherents of culture would traditionally disbelieve. Entry into this shadowy world "awaken[s] the mind's attention from the lethargy of custom" and strips the "film of familiarity" from our eyes (7, 2:7). But to gain admission to this imaginative world, the symbolist poet[2] and his readers must, by a heretical leap of faith, cross this shadow-line and pass beyond the culture's assumptions about the nature of reality. Once this heretical threshold is crossed, the symbolist poet frequently subverts the conventional images, symbols, language, or archetypes that collectively define the cultural episteme, for he or she has entered a landscape of chaos in which a new reality must be defined.

Surely all the poetry in *Lyrical Ballads,* whether Christian or heretical, aspires to freshness of perception. But Coleridge more than Wordsworth projects the modifying colors of imagination, and in so doing celebrates the power of the human mind to transform a universal object or image of the natural world into a personal symbol. Such symbols, or "involutions," as Coleridge calls them,[3] are the basis of the symbolist aesthetic, for they transmit a complex of personal emotional associations and derive their meaning from an autonomous human source. Coleridge's literary epistemology thus coincides closely with the symbolist vision of reality which embraces the imagination as a divine faculty (Daniel Schneider 1). From an epistemological standpoint, Coleridge's creative process subverts the culture's a priori sense of reality as revealed in conventional language, imagery, symbols, and archetypes. He entrusts his senses and imagination with the task of developing a personal apprehension of reality in which subject and object coalesce in the landscape created and inhabited by the poet.[4] The poet is thus responsible for a heretical cosmogeny in which the natural world of the Christian mythos is supplanted by a supernatural landscape that is the text of the poem.

It is not surprising, given their preoccupation with the way poetic landscape reveals the functioning mind, that Wordsworth and Coleridge and most of their contemporaries as well[5] should be so fond of the journey as a motif. The travel literature of the preceding century no doubt offered a model, for the Hebridean journals of Johnson and Boswell, the prose works of Swift and Defoe, and the novels of Smollett all raised questions about culture and self in relation to the "otherness" of foreign lands; they ventured into unfamiliar territory in the phenomenal world. It was quite natural, then, for romantic writers to create a new kind of physical and mental landscape where they could introduce fresh images in a symbolic geography. In this regard, Wordsworth's *Prelude,* according to romantic theorists, is of special significance because it offers a paradigm of the romantic circular journey. According to Northrop Frye's earliest theory, this archetypal model is based on a Christian prototype of a "gigantic cyclical myth, outlined in the Bible, which begins with the fall of man, is followed by a symbolic vision of human history, under the names of Adam and Israel, and ends with the redemption of Adam and Israel by Christ." Frye (1968) speculates that when "translated into Romantic terms, this myth assumes a quite different shape. What corresponds to the older myth of an unfallen state, or lost paradise of Eden, is now a sense of an original identity between individual man and nature which has been lost (17)." The romantic poet wished to reestablish this vital, sensuous connection by inducing fresh perception; consequently, the great romantic theme which emerges from this mythic sense of loss is a yearning for an "expanded consciousness [which brings about] the sense of identity with God and nature" (37). The circular journey, with its continual evocation of images and visionary moments, is the perfect vehicle for such expression.

M. H. Abrams further suggests that the romantic journey is a descendant of a biblical prototype such as the story of the prodigal son, in which the post-Adamic wanderer leaves his native land to journey through an alien land in quest of another, better land (*Natural Supernaturalism* 165). Though *The Prelude* is a good illustration of Abrams's model of the circuitous journey, when he extends his formula to the bulk of romantic poetry, including that of Coleridge, the paradigm is less appropriate. Other models have been proposed which more closely correspond to the symbolist voyage of disorientation. Bernard Blackstone in *The Lost Travellers* has distinguished between essentially circular Christian journeys and secularized versions that are more linear and move from "slum to garden" (10). Yet both of these journeys are teleological in that the wanderer reaches a goal which is an improvement of his initial, divided state. In a more comprehensive study, Roppen and Sommer argue that there are both teleological and nonteleological journeys that are respectively circular and linear. The first kind of journey, like that of *The Odyssey*, is controlled by a "circular progression toward renewal or restoration of the traveller-hero," while the second, similar to that of *The Aeneid*, is characterized by a "linear progression of the hero from a state of social or intellectual disorder toward one of order" (75). I propose a third kind of journey more basic to the symbolist tradition, a journey in which the wanderer or exile, despite what may appear to be a circular path, is never reborn, rejuvenated, or reintegrated into the society he has left. Neither is the journey an affirmative quest for self-knowledge since the awareness gained brings suffering and despair, usually unmitigated in the text itself. While the journeyer may experience what Praz has described as a characteristically romantic vacillation between hope and despair or joy and dejection, such vicissitudes do not give way to an affirmation of life, in the form of social reintegration, as some romantic theories hold. The traveler enters what may be termed a heretical space[6] whose chaos is characterized by a radical disorientation of the senses. The journeyer becomes permanently disoriented on a sensuous, psychological, and cultural level, so much so that the archetypal Christian return to a state of grace is either impossible or refused.[7]

Coleridge's "The Rime of the Ancient Mariner" is a controversial but paradigmatic example of such a heretical journey. The Mariner clearly travels a circular path, returning to his "native country," and experiences an archetypal death and rebirth within an explicitly Christian context. And yet there is ample evidence of disorientation and estrangement in the Mariner's experience and in the tenuous sense of closure offered by the moral of the poem.

The first stanzas of Coleridge's ballad are an exploration of the relationship between cultural symbology and individual perception. Of all social rituals, marriage is among those most clearly associated with the ratification and continuance of culture. A celebration of the union of two individuals, the marriage feast initiates a family into society and therefore extends as well as sanctifies the culture. The Mariner, who stands apart from this cultural, Christian celebration, is initially dismissed by the wedding guest as a "grey-beard loon" [11], until the "glittering eye" of the Mariner holds him spellbound. The initial situation of the poem thus implies a tension between the comfortable embracing of cultural values and the undeniable attraction of the visionary outcast who has gained an extraordinary knowledge that transcends and thereby implicitly challenges cultural perceptions. His power is compelling. Even though the wedding guest is "next of kin" to the wedding couple, "he cannot choose but hear" the story of the Mariner.

The poem continues to explore the relation between culture and perception as the Mariner begins his tale:

> The ship was cheered, the harbour cleared,
> Merrily did we drop
> Below the kirk, below the hill,
> Below the lighthouse top.
>
> [21–24]

After the townspeople cheer the Mariner's vessel in a communal sendoff, the emblems of the cultural order disappear as the ship sails below the horizon. Coleridge's mode of description is important, for the church and lighthouse, as obvious symbols of order and light, are not perceived as growing distant and gradually vanishing; rather, they drop out of sight abruptly as the poetic landscape switches to the heretical seascape described by the Mariner. The shift in perceptual mode as the ship drops below the church, below the hill, and below the lighthouse coincides with the beginning of the disorienting voyage.

Little need be added to Bodkin's classic discussion of the significance of descent with respect to the archetype of death and rebirth.[8] But it bears mention here because the disorienting symbolist voyage alternately adheres to and subverts traditional archetypal patterns that have been conventionalized in the Christian mythos. This vacillation between a passive adoption of cultural archetypes and the poet's active mythopoeic creation is discernible in "The Ancient Mariner," particularly in the mythic threshold the Mariner crosses and the unconventional seascape in which he subsequently travels. As the Mariner sails across the archetypal line, or equator, the symbolic geography of the poem reflects an immediate and pronounced transformation in the epistemology of the narrative, anticipated by the unusual description of the vanishing townscape. That change in epistemology, in the nature of what the Mariner sees and understands, marks a radical sensate disorientation that coincides with his departure from his native country and entry into a new seascape. Beyond the shadow-line, cultural knowledge is useless as a means of interpreting the phenomena the Mariner encounters:

> And now there came both mist and snow,
> And it grew wondrous cold:
> The ice, mast-high, came floating by,
> As green as emerald.
>
> And through the drifts the snowy clifts
> Did send a dismal sheen:
> Nor shapes of men nor beasts we ken—
> The ice was all between.
>
> The ice was here, the ice was there,
> The ice was all around:
> It cracked and growled, and roared and howled,
> Like noises in a swound!
>
> At length did cross an Albatross.
> Through the fog it came;
> As if it had been a Christian soul,
> We hailed it in God's name.
>
> [51–66]

In these four ballad stanzas, Coleridge introduces many of the salient characteristics of the disorienting voyage that expresses the modern heretical episteme, a world view at once part of and distinct from the gnostic traditions of Christian heresy which emphasize *gnosis* or self-knowledge gained through individual revelation (Grant 6–13) rather than belief through sacred scripture. The Mariner, like his heretical predecessors, depends less on any established cultural or religious symbol than on an individual, sensual manifestation of divinity; he derives knowledge from his individual percipience through his heightened visionary senses. Such heightened perceptions are initially evident in the Mariner's hyperesthetic sensations, his emphasis on the "wondrous cold" and his equal but opposite sensitivity to heat: "All in a hot and copper sky, / The bloody Sun" [111–12] beat down on the Mariner and crew "with broad and burning face" [180] so that "every tongue, through utter drought, / Was withered at the root" [135–36].

Though it is biographically uncertain whether Coleridge composed these verses after he had become addicted to opium or whether they were in fact composed, as Lowes argues, predominantly from secondary sources and the modifying colors of imagination,[9] it is clear that the hypersensitivity of the tactile sense is akin to that of the opium addict (Hayter 44). This is an important point, for the convention of the disorienting voyage of modern symbolist literature has for its precedent not only heretical mysticism but also the drug-induced sensate disorientation of writers like Coleridge and De Quincey.[10] This visual and tactile sensitivity in part produces the synesthetic interplay of sense qualities that, like his hyperesthesia, defines the extraordinary nature of the Mariner's experience. The emerald-green ice floats by "mast-high," a visual and kinesthetic combination which suggests an icy, emerald ship sailing in an otherworldly seascape.

In such totally unfamiliar surroundings, defined by senses that are supersensitive, synesthetically correspondent, or confused, the Mariner and crew see neither "shapes of men nor beasts [they] ken." And yet, before the Mariner's eyes, the phenomenal world comes alive: "It cracked and growled, and roared and howled, / Like noises in a swound!" Such animism is a typical component of the journey into heretical space. The

Mariner's seascape is a confusion of cold and hot, water and thirst, life and death, all of which is animated and ordered by the mythopoeic imagination of the poet-narrator, and reanimated and retold by the Mariner. Such mythopoeic animism necessarily challenges the cultural sense of reality. Disavowing or withdrawing from the Christian universe, the visionary heretic creates a new landscape out of the chaos of the senses. As the Mariner disjoins the cultural episteme by entering a landscape where all is uncharted, he becomes entirely disoriented; he can depend on no predetermined reality, nothing known before. Hence, the sensate derangement experienced by the Mariner (the "noises in a swound") indicates a simultaneous epistemological and cultural disorientation. His swoon marks another threshold of consciousness in which his imaginative voyage is the only universe that exists.

These sensate derangements give way to the near cessation of all sense stimuli during the Mariner's anesthetic life-in-death that occurs later in the narrative. Again, little need be added to Bodkin's discussion of the archetypal significance of this section of the poem except that the spectres and demons which dominate Parts 3–4 anticipate the spectral persecution that is common in the heretical works of literature examined in the present study. Such spectres and ghosts stand in opposition to those of orthodox Christian symbology. Most obviously, the use of the symbol of the albatross, to represent either the Christian soul or Christ himself, is an idiosyncratic and therefore iconoclastic subversion of Christian symbolism. Even to this day, the image of an albatross around one's neck carries no specifically religious connotation but is rather an emblem of the guilt-ridden pariah who is interested less in crimes against God than in crimes punishable by the self. It is thus the mythopoetic imagination of the poet which conjures polar spirits, the "Spectre-woman and her Death-mate"; the poet depends little on preexisting symbols, myths, or cultural archetypes.

In keeping with the convention of the dream vision and the Christian paradigm of descent and return, however, the Mariner begins an archetypal return after blessing the water snakes.

The marginal gloss at line 378 again locates the Mariner at the "Line," which, when crossed, induces another swoon [392] that serves as a return threshold. Coleridge has thus created a roughly symmetrical structure through the formal repetition of images or narrative events:

Meeting with wedding guest [1–20]
  Communal cheering of ship in native country [21]
    Ship reaches the line [30]
      Hyperesthesia, sense disorientation, swoon [50–62]
     Destruction of Christian soul
     Life-in-death
    Spectral persecution
   Vision of angelic spirits [350–72]
  Recrossing the line, swoon [380–92]
 Hermit cheers ship returned to native country [528]
Frame meeting with wedding guest [580–625]

There seems little reason to doubt, given this formal pattern, that Coleridge intended to portray an archetypal death and rebirth within a specifically Christian framework. Simply stated, the Mariner commits an inexplicable transgression, saves his soul by blessing God's creatures, and remains penitent for his sin. Yet there are a number of ways in which "The Ancient Mariner" departs from the paradigm of the romantic circular journey.

First, the symmetry of events in the structure of the journey is undercut by a powerful formal disorientation that is characteristic of the symbolist voyage. That formal disorientation, extending beyond the imagistic disorientation of hyperesthesia or synesthesia, becomes a kind of disorganizing principle reflected in linguistic or structural disorientation. In "The Ancient Mariner," linguistic and structural disjunctions are created by the simultaneous presentation of poetry and marginal glosses. Though Coleridge published the glosses some twenty years after the original composition of the work (1797, 1817), the poem is well known for its two coincidental texts. The presence of two parallel texts disorients the reader, particularly the first-time reader, whose attention is divided between them. Morse Peckham has identified this disorganizing concept as central to all romantic poetry which, he claims, was a reaction against the "epistemological inadequacy" of the eighteenth century:

> Tension between subject and object was the truth of the matter, they were convinced, and hence the task of the artist was to create a perceptual field to which psychological adaptation was anything but easy, a field which would permit and require and force the artistic observer to experience perceptual and cognitive disorientation and in grasping that field to engage the power of the creative imagination. (21)

Even though Coleridge and his critics have generally thought of "The Ancient Mariner" as poetic text with an incidental gloss, the coincidental texts exert mutual influence on each other and create the perceptual and cognitive disorientation of which Peckham speaks. On its most basic level this disorientation occurs in the disruption of the physical process of reading; the eye is forced to move from right to left as well as left to right, and up as well as down on the page. The result is a linguistic subversion, in which the reader's attention is divided between competing narratives. When the reader makes a leap between texts, he or she effectively crosses the shadow-line that Coleridge refers to in the *Biographia*, for the two narratives are not of the same order of reality.[11] The prose gloss and poetic text offer two separate mentalities, one a rational, "civilized scholastic voice" (Lipking 614) and the other a superrational, imaginative poetic utterance. In a sense, then, the poem expresses two competing epistemologies, one embodied in a supernatural and heretical poem and the other in an essentially Christian prose gloss explaining what the culturally competent reader might otherwise find incomprehensible or unbelievable in the poem. This epistemological tension thus creates a kind of schizophrenic disorientation in the reading process. As Lipking asserts, the "pious idiom" of the gloss "invests [it] with an aura of unproblematical faith, of certain knowledge" (619), all of which is simultaneously called into question by the incomprehensible wilderness of the seascape. What results is a "tension between the two ways of construing the mariner's tale—between experiencing it and interpreting it" (621).

A second important question that I wish to raise pertains to the Mariner's greeting upon his return. Why is the otherwise perfect circularity of the journey broken when the Mariner is cheered not by the general community but by the Hermit good? Truly, the Hermit is portrayed as a holy man to whom the Mariner turns for penance; yet the Hermit is himself a voluntary exile from society who "loves to talk with Mariners / That come from a far countree" (517–18). The religious observance of human isolation as a mark of holiness is, perhaps inadvertently, called into question by the hellish isolation of the Mariner during his life-in-death experience and by the overall context of a tale told to a wedding guest who is trying to join a celebration feast. Had the Mariner been greeted and cheered by the general public, it would have made a far less interesting poem but one that more clearly fits the symmetrical Christian paradigm of a circular return to grace and order. Instead, the Mariner fails to respond to the cheer offered by a social exile and enters a state of exile much more dreadful than that of the Hermit:

> Since then, at an uncertain hour,
> That agony returns:
> And till my ghastly tale is told,
> This heart within me burns.
>
> I pass, like night, from land to land;
> I have strange power of speech;
> That moment that his face I see,
> I know the man that must hear me:
> To him my tale I teach.
>
> [582–90]

Using the story of the wandering Jew, Coleridge invokes the biblical punishment of wandering (Anderson 11–15) and simultaneously admits the appropriateness of secular myth. This invocation of the heretical wanderer, for whom there is no hope of cultural rootedness, marks what may be Coleridge's inadvertent admission that orthodox faith is not *simply* triumphant in the case of the Mariner. The Mariner experiences less a sense of reunion with God than a profound sense of knowing he has visited a landscape "so lonely . . . that God himself / Scarce seemed there to be" [599–600]. And the knowledge of his disorienting journey, as well as the guilt he feels for having destroyed a Christian soul, sends him into permanent exile. The Mariner is one condemned to wander forever on the fringe of society, on the periphery of wedding feasts, in order to retell his harrowing, and heretical, story. The conclusion of "The Ancient Mariner" may thus reflect the weakening of faith and the troubling religious skepticism that Coleridge himself felt during the years surrounding the writing of the poem (Barth 1969, 1–13).

Coleridge's "Ancient Mariner" thus offers a seminal paradigm defining the relationship between sense perception and the modern heretical vision. In this pattern, the journeyer typically crosses a threshold and enters an animistic realm characterized by a hyperesthetic, synesthetic, or anesthetic derangement of the senses, which is reflected in the unorthodox images, language, or structure of the work. This disorientation of the senses induces an altered awareness of self and subverts the cultural episteme, that a priori sense of what is culturally known or knowable. This altered knowledge renders the journeyer a permanent exile from his or her own culture, without hope of regeneration or return.

Two
Thomas De Quincey's Defect of the Eye

> *This is the doctrine of the true church on the subject of opium: of which church I acknowledge myself to be the Pope (consequently infallible).*
> —Thomas De Quincey, *Confessions of an English Opium-Eater*

The autobiographical writings and prose fantasies of Thomas De Quincey offer the clearest, if not the first, alternative to the Wordsworthian tradition. This is not to say that De Quincey sought a radical break from the influence of his predecessor; if anything, De Quincey thought of himself as a disciple and venerated the poet laureate until their gradual falling out after De Quincey's return to Grasmere in 1810. Even then, De Quincey thought of their estrangement as more personal and temperamental than literary, so powerful was Wordsworth's sway on De Quincey's conscious literary opinions. Despite this acknowledged affinity, one finds in De Quincey's writings a distinct if unconscious departure from the poetic landscapes of Wordsworth. The journeys of De Quincey, like those of Coleridge, are voyages of disorientation that sever the journeyer from both nature and God.[1] De Quincey's narrators make linear voyages that end in the opium-inspired, labyrinthine realm of the pariah. In *Confessions of an English Opium-Eater*, *Suspiria de Profundis*, and *The English Mail-Coach*, De Quincey journeys away from Wordsworthian inno-

---

Portions of this chapter are taken from *Thomas De Quincey: Bicentenary Studies*, edited and with an introduction by Robert Lance Snyder. Copyright © 1985 by the University of Oklahoma Press.

References to *Suspiria de Profundis* are from *De Quincey's Writings*, Vol. 1, Boston: Ticknor, Reed, and Fields (1851). References to *Confessions of an English Opium-Eater* and other works by De Quincey are from *The Collected Writings of Thomas De Quincey*, Ed. David Masson, 14 Vols. London: A.C. Black, 1896.

cence into a heretical space in which he celebrates disorientation from the normal sensate, social, and divine worlds.

Departure from the Wordsworthian Landscape

The journey motif which provides a structure for the first section of De Quincey's *Confessions* is, in one respect, conventionally literary; the departure from Manchester, the walking tour of Wales, and the entry into London derive both from the travel literature of the preceding century (De Quincey mentions Boswell and Johnson by name) and from the contemporary use of the journey as a metaphor for the evolution of the author's mind. But in an important way, this evolution is unlike the Wordsworthian "growth of the poet's mind" in *The Prelude*. Though De Quincey, like Wordsworth, recounts his earliest recollections of childhood, those recollections focus on his determinate, linear path from being an orphan at the age of seven to his downfall in London and his hellish existence as an opium-eater. That journey is defined by a landscape colored by the imagination of the mature opium addict. Unlike the Christian journey of Wordsworth, which attempts to recover or approximate an earlier blessed state, De Quincey's journey marks a departure from what is socially acceptable and what is culturally sanctioned and known. Once the pathway is established, there is no possibility of a Wordsworthian return to a state of social integration, grace, or joy, whether real, recollected, or intimated.

The conscious literary symbolism that De Quincey employs is evident in his sense of "going forth" from the Manchester Grammar School in July of 1802. The occasion marked not only his liberation from the confines of school and familial guardianship, but also his being "launch[ed] . . . into the world" (1896, 3:294). The seventeen-year-old De Quincey dreams ominously in his Manchester study of his past and future when a voice, seemingly audible, warns him, "'Once leave this house, and a Rubicon is placed between thee and all possibility of return'" (1896, 3:297). In retrospect, De Quincey interprets his going forth as an irrevocable passage into another realm of life experience that his socially conditioned conscience cannot sanction. His conscious articulation decades later is, of course, colored by subsequent experience and a likely desire to replicate the innocence of childhood. Yet, asserting his own literary independence from Wordsworth, De Quincey declares that he knew that he must leave his protected situation, begin his life's journey, and enter a permanent state of exile.

During the travel sequences early in the *Confessions,* De Quincey indulges in his characteristic melodrama. Portraying his journey as both personal and allegorical, De Quincey transforms the Welsh countryside into an overtly symbolic landscape divided from the anthropomorphized London:

> All through the day, Wales and her grand mountain ranges . . . had divided my thoughts with London. But now rose London—sole, dark, infinite—brooding over the whole capacities of my heart. . . . More than ever I stood upon the brink of a precipice; and the local circumstances around me deepened and intensified these reflections, impressed upon them solemnity and terror, sometimes even horror. (3:346)

The resemblance between the reported experience of young De Quincey and the voyage of the Ancient Mariner is apparent in the boundary that marks the threshold of the extraordinary experience De Quincey will have in London. Like the Ancient Mariner, the young De Quincey will undergo an epistemological transformation as the "local circumstances," the domestic scenery which besieges the eye, induce the hyperesthetic and deranged sensations characteristic of heretical space:

> The unusual dimensions of the rooms, especially their towering height, brought up continually and obstinately, through natural links of associated feelings or

> images, the mighty vision of London waiting for me afar off.... This single feature of the rooms—their unusual altitude, and the echoing hollowness which had become the exponent of that altitude—this one terrific feature (for terrific it was in the effect), together with crowding and evanescent images of the flying feet that so often had spread gladness through these halls on the wings of youth and hope at seasons when every room rang with music: all this, rising in tumultuous vision, whilst the dead hours of night were stealing along,—all around me, household and town, sleeping,—and whilst against the windows more and more the storm outside was raving, and to all appearance endlessly growing,—threw me into the deadliest condition of nervous emotion under contradictory forces, high over which predominated horror recoiling from that unfathomable abyss in London into which I was now so wilfully precipitating myself. (3:346–47)

The "natural links of associated feelings and images" create both synesthesia and hyperesthesia, the dominant literary techniques of the passage. The vertiginous height of the room's ceiling produces auditory effects which in turn trigger a "tumultuous vision." Normal sense perception is suspended and replaced by an imaginative disorientation. Having crossed a heretical threshold, De Quincey describes the moment when the socially conditioned self is destroyed and, with it, any a priori sense of reality. Like the seascape of the Ancient Mariner, the chamber and landscape in Shrewsbury seem to vibrate animistically as the storm "raves" outside: "Wild it was beyond all description, and dark as 'the inside of a wolf's throat.'" In these surroundings and amid the violent sensate disorientation, De Quincey reemphasizes the boundary he has crossed: "Still, as I turned inwards to the echoing chambers, or outwards to the wild, wild night, I saw London expanding her visionary gates to receive me, like some dreadful mouth of Acheron" (3:347). His symbolic journey complete, De Quincey descends into the hellish abyss of London and opium addiction.

The Subversion of Archetypes

After the section treating his allegorical journey to London, De Quincey's *Confessions* are divided into two parts, the "Pleasures" and the "Pains" of opium. When De Quincey divides his career as an opium-eater into two phases, he transforms the earlier physical journey into archetypal, mental landscapes. Moreover, this division indicates the continuing evolution of his mind and his reasoned attempt to define the personal and literary importance of his opium experiences. Now on a mental journey, De Quincey seeks, in Alethea Hayter's words, to understand "the way in which dreams and visions are formed, how opium helps to form them and intensifies them, and how they are then recomposed and used in conscious art" (103). His opium reveries and particularly his hypnagogic visions are responsible for transmuting dreams into patterns of thought and expressions of the literary imagination, which finally become part of the landscapes of his prose "dream-fugues" (113). During this process of reconstituting dreams into symbolic landscapes, De Quincey's mythopoeic imagination often subverts the cultural episteme by re-forming traditional archetypes to meet the demands of his personal symbology. In the *Confessions*, this is most apparent in his reconstitution of the Christian archetypes of heaven and hell as the pleasures and pains of opium. The body of images associated with these two states of mind reflects his conflicted sense of reality. De Quincey is drawn to the pleasures of opium and the accompanying sense of tranquil equilibrium associated with the Christian episteme, and at the same time he is fascinated with the pains of opium and the resulting sensate disorientation associated with the symbolist, heretical episteme.

As De Quincey recounts his early stages of addiction to the "celestial drug," he quickly counters what he thought was a common, contemporary misconception about the use of laudanum, or opium, that opium-eating made the user sluggish, torpid, or antisocial. De Quincey argues that, at least in the initial stages of addiction, opium stimulated the intellect and inclined him toward attending social functions, particularly the opera. He also counters the argument that opium promoted the loss of moral sensibility or self-command. Such loss of control often results from overindulgence in alcohol, he notes, but opium introduces the most exquisite harmony and order to the mental faculties (1896, 3:382–96). In his finest hours of pleasure De Quincey reports:

> it seemed to me as if then first I stood at a distance aloof from the uproar of life; as if the tumult, the fever, and the strife, were suspended; a respite were granted from the secret burdens of the heart; some Sabbath of repose; some resting from human labours. Here were the hopes which blossom in the paths of life, reconciled with the peace which is in the grave; motions of the intellect as unwearied as the heavens, yet for all anxieties a halcyon calm; tranquillity that seemed no product of inertia, but as if resulting from mighty and equal antagonisms; infinite activities, infinite repose. (1896, 3:395)

During those early stages of use when De Quincey still found opium pleasurable, he experienced "halcyon" states of mind that are overtly compared to the Christian "Sabbath" or "heaven." This is particularly true during his prospect reveries, such as his vision while surveying the Irish Sea, a passage that reads much like a Wordsworthian "spot of time":

> At that time I often fell into such reveries after taking opium . . . when I have been seated at an open window, from which I could overlook the sea at a mile below me, and could at the same time command a view of some great town standing on a different radius of my circular prospect, but at nearly the same distance—that from sunset to sunrise, all through the hours of night, I have continued motionless, as if frozen, without consciousness of myself as of an object anywise distinct from the multiform scene which I contemplated from above. (1896, 3:394–95)

The stamp of Wordsworth is clear. The speaker is "laid asleep in body" during a wedding of the "majestic intellect" with the natural world, an experience recollected later in tranquility.

But here and elsewhere in De Quincey's work, there is an important distinction between the prospect reveries of Wordsworth and his one-time disciple. Rejecting the journey through a landscape that reflects the poetic mind, De Quincey is often engaged in a visionary experience indoors, typically as he looks outdoors through a perceptual frame. This disjunction from the natural world is accompanied by a strong undertone of suppressed sorrow that is inconsistent with the Wordsworthian moment:

> Obliquely to the left lay the many-languaged town of Liverpool; obliquely to the right, the multitudinous sea. . . . The town of Liverpool represented the earth, with its sorrows and its graves left behind, yet not out of sight, nor wholly forgotten. The ocean, in everlasting but gentle agitation, yet brooded over by dove-like calm, might not unfitly typify the mind, and the mood which then swayed it. (1896, 3:395)

While this scene reminds one of Wordsworth's ascent of Mt. Snowdon at the end of *The Prelude* or his reflections on the "still, sad music of humanity" as he gazes down on the sylvan Wye, De Quincey's seascapes (and landscapes), viewed under the influence of the pains of opium, have a more ominous, agitating undercurrent.

Such scenes of apparent tranquility are drastically changed during the later stages of addiction. If during the pleasures of opium the sea and lake scenes evoke a Wordsworthian tranquility and harmony characteristic of the Christian episteme, during the pains of opium such scenes are broken down and replaced with disorienting visions that well from the disturbed mythopoeic consciousness of De Quincey:

> The waters gradually changed their character—from translucent lakes, shining like mirrors, they became seas and oceans. And now came a tremendous change,

> which, unfolding itself slowly like a scroll, through many months, promised an abiding torment. . . . Hitherto the human face had often mixed in my dreams, but not despotically. . . . But now that affection which I have called the tyranny of the human face began to unfold itself. . . . My mind tossed, as it seemed, upon the billowy ocean, and weltered upon the weltering waves. (1896, 3:441)

It was the opium experience that allowed De Quincey to move beyond the cultural decorations of civilized landscapes and descend into the realm of racial consciousness. Anticipating the archetypal psychologists of our present century, De Quincey refers, in an early version of *Suspiria de Profundis,* to his troubling visions and dreams as the "abysses of aboriginal fear and eldest darkness" (1851, 196). Conceiving such fears in a Christian context, De Quincey likens the visions to a reliving of the fall and expulsion from paradise: "In dreams, perhaps under some secret conflict of the midnight sleeper, lighted up to the consciousness at the time, but darkened to the memory as soon as all is finished, each several child of our mysterious race completes for himself the treason of the aboriginal fall" (1896, 13:304). Though expressed in Christian terms, the thrust of De Quincey's idea and the experience it describes is essentially psychological and involves individual, isolated participation. Though the heretical vision may take place in the company of others, communality of vision is impossible. Each may experience it, according to De Quincey, but few attempt to articulate it or embrace it as a viable mode of perception. Most return to the comfortable perceptions of the community.

Mechanical Models of Mind

De Quincey's assertion that such heretical visions are "darkened to the memory" provides us with the key to the relationship between dreaming, opium, and De Quincey's literary imagination. The epistemology that emerges from his discussion centers on the traditional romantic connection between the senses and the imagination and yet is based equally on an original conception of the dreaming mind as outlined in *Suspiria:*

> The machinery for dreaming planted in the human brain was not planted for nothing. That faculty, in alliance with the mystery of darkness, is the one great tube through which man communicates with the shadowy. And the dreaming organ, in connection with the heart, the eye, and the ear, compose the magnificent apparatus which forces the infinite into the chambers of a human brain. (1851, 149)

It is this basic tenet of De Quincey's epistemology that led him to adopt various formal mechanisms, all clearly analogues of opium intoxication, that offer a distinct alternative to the Wordsworthian perceptual mode. Furthermore, when these analogous mechanisms are understood within the context of childhood experience, or "nursery experiences," as De Quincey calls them, we see even more clearly how De Quincey's epistemology questions cultural attitudes toward innocence and perception.

In his writing, De Quincey challenges the traditional cultural association of childhood innocence with a state of divine grace. De Quincey modifies Wordsworth's theory of a prelapsarian childhood state by investing his own nursery experiences with images of intoxication, sensations garnered from his addiction to opium. Unlike Wordsworth, who maintained that "the human mind is capable of excitement without the application of gross and violent stimulants" (Wordsworth 21), De Quincey, in *Suspiria,* rhetorically compares the freshness of perception in childhood with the hyperesthetic imagery of the opium addict's landscape: "The nursery experience had been the ally and the natural coefficient of the opium. For that reason it was that the nursery experience has been narrated. Logically, it bears the very same relation to the convulsions of the dreaming faculty as the opium" (1851, 223). In the autobiographical literature, the infant De Quincey is portrayed by the adult author as experiencing various kinds of disorientation during childhood which facilitate his visions. More than Coleridge's modifying colors of imagination, De Quincey's apparatus are dynamic, disorienting structures, lenses or mechanisms which intensify and distort infant experience so that it more closely resembles his mature, adult visions.

De Quincey's most important experience of childhood disorientation comes in the whispering gallery of St. Paul's Cathedral in London. For De Quincey the gallery expresses the interrelation of childhood experience, the journey of life, and sensual disorientation. It is a metaphorical involute; that is, it is an event or object surrounded by a complex of emotional associations. In the *Autobiography,* he writes: "I am struck with the truth, that far more of our deepest thoughts and feelings pass to us as . . . *involutes* (if I may coin that word) in compound experiences incapable of being disentangled" (1896, 1:39), and later suggests that such involutes are "combinations in which the materials of future thought or feeling are carried . . . into the mind" (1896, 1:128). Unlike Coleridge who uses the term "involution" to suggest the transformation of a universal truth into an individual one,[2] De Quincey treats involutes as a series of discrete seminal experiences that become inextricably bound together and that recur in our associative consciousness. Thus, for De Quincey, the gallery represents both the continuity and discontinuity of life experience (Blake 639). It is an emblem of continuity because a whispered utterance travels in a circular path from one end to the other, but it becomes a metaphor of discontinuity when De Quincey, perhaps mistakenly, contends that the original utterance is grotesquely transformed. Since De Quincey suggests that the mechanism involves a hyperesthetic transformation of sensation, the whispering gallery itself becomes something like a model of mind, or conscience, and an analogue to opium intoxication:

> Thou, also, Whispering Gallery! once again in those moments of conscious and wilful desolation didst to my ear utter monitorial sighs. For once again I was prepar-

ing to utter an irrevocable word, to enter upon one of those fatally tortuous paths of which the windings can never be unlinked. (1896, 3:347)

A clear echo of the Shrewsbury hotel sequence, this passage establishes a determinate link between youthful experience and adult addiction. De Quincey thus found a perfect symbolist involute: the coalescence of intense personal emotion, powerful sense experience, and a solemn truth about opium-eating. This association becomes fixed in De Quincey's imagination, for he makes the same literary association when discussing the implications of his journeying forth from the Manchester Grammar School: "'Thou wilt not say that what thou doest is altogether approved in thy secret heart. Even now thy conscience speaks against it in sullen whispers; but at the other end of thy long life-gallery that same conscience will speak to thee in volleying thunders'" (1896, 3:297). As an involute, the gallery becomes an associative complex of deranged sensation, deterministic action, and guilt:

> [The] sentiment of nervous recoil from any word or deed that could not be recalled had been suddenly reawakened . . . by the impressive experience of the Whispering Gallery. At the earlier end of the gallery had stood my friend, breathing in the softest whispers a solemn but not acceptable truth. At the further end, after running along the walls of the gallery, that solemn truth reached me as a deafening menace in tempestuous uproars. (1896, 3:296)

In both Manchester Grammar School and the Shrewsbury hotel sequences, De Quincey compares his emerging disorientation from society to an earlier extraordinary sense experience and, in his own mind, sees the journey of his life as fated. There is thus a clear and compelling connection between hyperesthetic sensation and the break from social convention, an estrangement that will be relived in his experience as an opium-eater.

This relationship between childhood experience and the tortured path that led to his adult addiction to opium preoccupies

De Quincey throughout his writing career. In his *Autobiography*, De Quincey struggles with his desire to celebrate the child as an autonomous self enjoying "rural seclusion" in the "silent garden" of Greenhay (1896, 1:34) and his psychological need to integrate his adult and childhood selves: "An adult sympathizes with himself in childhood because he *is* the same, and because (being the same) yet he is *not* the same. He acknowledges the deep, mysterious identity between himself, as adult and as infant, for the ground of his sympathy; and yet, ... he feels the differences between his two selves as the main quickeners of his sympathy" (1851, 154–55). Again, the disorienting structure of the whispering gallery comes to mind: the uttered "monitorial sighs" of childhood *are* and *are not* the same sounds that reach the adult conscience as "tempestuous uproars." While there is a Wordsworthian sympathy between adult and child, the childhood experience is hardly recollected in tranquility. In the opening paragraph of Chapter 4 of *The Autobiography*, De Quincey further suggests how his notion of childhood and adult experiences differs from that of Wordsworth:

> 'The Child,' says Wordsworth, '*is father of the man*'; thus calling into conscious notice the fact ... that whatsoever is seen in the maturest adult ... must have pre-existed by way of germ in the infant.... But not, therefore, is it true inversely—that all which pre-exists in the child finds its development in the man.... Most of what he has, the grown-up man inherits from his infant self; but it does not follow that he always enters upon the whole of his natural inheritance. (1896, 1:121)

This "quickening of sympathy" and the development of preexistent childhood qualities in the mature adult invite the adult De Quincey to portray his younger self as a precocious participant in the "horror of life [which] mixed itself ... in earliest youth with the heavenly sweetness of life" (1851, 257). As this mixture is analogous to the pleasures and pains of opium, De Quincey applies the concept of spiritual disorientation to his early life experience and the emergence of consciousness.

De Quincey adopts the imagery of disorientation, even for his early nursery experiences, to suggest the fragmentary, discontinuous nature of his divided but potentially integrated childhood and adult selves (Blake 635). He depicts this mixture of selves through the visionary experiences of a precocious child, whose self-conscious visions, through a disorienting pictorial frame,[3] transcend the limits of normal, adult perception. In order to achieve a comparable sense of spiritual transcendence as an adult, De Quincey induced a state of sensate derangement, via opium, in which his normal, cultural perceptions could be abandoned. Through this kind of sensual derangement, De Quincey found an idiom for describing his adult experiences, an idiom which demanded a lens of disorientation that would eventually become a mechanism for introducing similar experiences into his sympathetic nursery experiences.

Many of De Quincey's devices that induce sensate disequilibrium are visual lenses that metaphorically or actually distort the perceptual field. For example, in his *Diary,* he imagines himself "looking through a glass" and seeing a man in a "dim and shadowy perspective and (as it were) in a dream" (156). This kind of visually disorienting moment during De Quincey's adolescence and early childhood is important because it is metaphorically connected with the visionary imagination. In *Suspiria,* when he describes the death of his sister, visual disorientation plays a critical role in shaping a reality that transcends ordinary perception:

> Into the woods or the desert air I gazed as if some comfort lay hid in *them.* I wearied the heavens with my inquest of beseeching looks. I tormented the blue depths with obstinate scrutiny, sweeping them with my eyes, and searching them for ever after one angelic face that might perhaps have permission to reveal itself for a moment. The faculty of shaping images in the distance after the yearnings of the heart, aided by a slight defect in my eyes,[4] grew upon me at this time. And I recall at the

present moment one instance of that sort, which may show how merely shadows, or a gleam of brightness, or nothing at all, could furnish a sufficient basis for this creative faculty. (1851, 184)

The images that De Quincey shapes "after the yearnings of the heart" are happily distorted by a "defect" in his eyes. It is unclear whether De Quincey refers to his myopia, apparently rather severe, or to an inflammation of the eye which occasionally troubled him.[5] Whatever its cause, in the early, unrevised "Affliction," De Quincey embraces the defect, or what he calls in the *Confessions* a "mechanic affection of the eye," (1896, 3:434) as a means of engaging and exciting the imaginative, visionary faculties. His welcoming of the visual dysfunction is a willed derangement of the senses analogous to the opium experience.

The phenomenon of sense disorientation inducing the child's visionary moment is clearly demonstrated in *Suspiria* by the vision of grief and death De Quincey projects in church when he mourns the loss of his sister: "Raising my streaming eyes to the windows of the galleries, [I] saw, on days when the sun was shining, a spectacle as affecting as ever prophet can have beheld." His blurred vision deepens the "purples and crimsons" through which "streamed the golden light" and intensifies the "emblazonries of heavenly illumination mingling with earthly emblazonries" (1851, 185). Because of its mechanical nature, this imaginative flight is thought by some critics to be "inadequate" as a visionary experience (De Luca 67), but the vision is intense and does explore the relation of life and death to the finite and the infinite (Bruss 98):

> I saw through the wide central field of the window, where the glass was uncolored, white fleecy clouds sailing over the azure depths of the sky; were it but a fragment or a hint of such a cloud, immediately under the flash of my sorrow-haunted eye, it grew and shaped itself into a vision of beds with white lawny curtains; and in the beds lay sick children, dying children, that

were tossing with anguish, and weeping clamorously for death. (1851, 185–86)

De Quincey's perceptive and cognitive frame is suddenly disoriented, disrupted by the "flash" of his eye which projects, through an artificial lens, the transcendent vision of anguish and death, a vision that might well have been the product of the pains of opium but one that clearly seems beyond the ken of a six-year-old.[6]

There are other visionary moments in the nursery experiences of De Quincey which are described through opium imagery, but none is so vividly portrayed or so explicitly associated with the drug as his trancelike vision as he stands over the corpse of his sister: "Whilst I stood, a solemn wind began to blow, the most mournful that ear ever heard. . . . It was a wind that had swept the fields of mortality for a hundred centuries" (1851, 175). This experience becomes a De Quincean involute which, exciting both auditory and visual images, prompts the visionary experience: "Instantly, when my ears caught this vast Aeolian intonation, when my eye filled with the golden fullness of life, . . . instantly a trance fell upon me. A vault seemed to open in the zenith of the far blue sky, a shaft which ran up for ever" (1896, 176). The adult interpolation of the childhood vision appears in the expanded consciousness of a child who conceives of a "hundred centuries" and who witnesses the infinite expansion of space. These hyperesthetic distortions are identical to the intoxicating effects of opium. The young De Quincey, in effect, has an opium vision.

As if sensing this imposition of adult experience, De Quincey compares the contraction of time in his recent childish vision to the elastic expansion of time experienced under the influence of opium:

But why speak of [the vision] in connection with opium? Could a child of six years old have been under that influence? No, but simply because it so exactly reversed the operation of opium. Instead of a short interval expanding into a vast one, upon this occasion a long one had contracted into a minute . . . during this wandering or suspension of my perfect mind. (1851, 177)

Despite his disclaimer, De Quincey describes both time and space in his vision as expansive: intonations are vast, the vault into the heavens runs up forever, and these hyperesthetic exaggerations seem "to go on for ever and ever." The fact that these descriptions are part of a mental landscape that De Quincey had not yet inhabited is less important than what they tell us about De Quincey's motivation for writing and about the fictionalizing process of his autobiographical works. The nursery and adolescent experiences are an account of his adult experiences of pleasure and pain grafted onto the events of childhood. As such, they seek to explain the origins of his addiction as grief coupled with a precocious but "constitutional determination to reverie" (1851, 147); at the same time they tend to naturalize and sanctify the adult addiction to the "celestial drug" (1896, 3:381), thereby lessening the older De Quincey's poignant sense of guilt and social disorientation.

In De Quincey's adult life, too, there are experiences which mimic the intoxication and disorientation induced by opium. One such example can be found in "The English Mail-Coach." The reader's perceptual frame is most obviously distorted by the narrator's opium-inspired imagery: the driver's metamorphosis into a cyclops, the narrator's heightened sensitivity to sights and sounds, and his exaggeration of time and space just before the coach nearly collides with the lovers' gig. But the coach is also a disorienting apparatus which compels a synesthetic view of reality. Through the coach, De Quincey celebrates the "glory of motion" and the kinesthetic sense invades virtually all the perceptive faculties: the velocity of the coach provides "grand effects for the eye between lamp-light and the darkness upon solitary roads" (1896, 13:271) and even enables the narrator to hear the sound of motion some four miles distant (1896, 13:311). De Quincey thus exploits opium intoxication for the formal purpose of disorienting the reader through synesthesia, transferal of sense experience (hearing motion), and manipulation of narrative pace through the cognitive disorientation.

De Quincey, narrating that he sits atop the mail-coach beside the slumbering coachman who has been metamorphosed into a cyclops, is fully under the spell of opium and has "yielded to the influence of the mighty calm [so] as to sink into a profound reverie" (1896, 13:310). But the dreamlike state is broken by the first hints of impending disaster:

> Suddenly . . . I was awakened to a sullen sound, as of some motion on the distant road. . . . Once roused, however, I could not but observe with alarm the quickened motion of our horses. Ten years' experience had made my eye learned in the valuing of motion; and I saw that we were now running thirteen miles an hour. . . . Again the far-off sound of a wheel was heard! A whisper it was—a whisper from, perhaps, four miles off. (1896, 13:311–12)

In the near darkness and moving down the road, De Quincey experiences a sympathetic synesthesia; he does not merely hear the sound of the distant carriage, he hears its motion, faintly and reportedly from a distance of four miles. (The mail-coach is still some fifteen minutes from overtaking the unknown vehicle.) This hyperesthesia, imagined though it may be, is based on a kinesthetic sense of hearing, which has taken over in the absence of vision, which under normal circumstances would have informed those on the coach of the distance to the vehicle ahead.

Just as he distorts the visual, aural, and kinesthetic senses, De Quincey also psychologically stretches the sense of time, a distortion that has much the same effect as the linguistic disorientation created by the competing texts of "The Ancient Mariner." In De Quincey, the reading process is subverted by the competition between the story line and plotted digression.[7] De Quincey narrates that as the mail-coach rapidly approaches the vehicle, he is horrified by his inability to act. To accomplish a mimetic poesis between text and psychological state, De Quincey disorients the reader by manipulating the pace of the narrative to elasticize the sense of temporal progress. When the vehicle ahead is first described as coming into view, De Quincey begins his digression with a hyperesthetic attention to the detail of his surroundings: "Before us lay an avenue straight as an arrow, six hundred yards, perhaps, in length; and the umbrageous trees, which rose in a regular line from either side, meeting high overhead, gave to it the character of a cathedral aisle" (1896, 13:313–14). With his path and speed determined, De Quincey carefully informs the reader that only about one-and-a-half minutes travel time separates the vehicles. Unable to slow the runaway horses or sound the carriage's horn, the "opium-shattered" narrator reports he shouted two unheard warnings. De Quincey, the master of digression, takes this particular opportunity to reflect on how his action is illuminated by the *Aeneid*. De Quincey thus playfully sidetracks the reader's attention with gratuitous narration and simultaneously compels the reader to be alert to the impending collision. At the end of two long paragraphs, about two minutes of reading time, twenty fictional seconds have elapsed. De Quincey continues:

> For seven seconds, it might be, of his seventy, [before a potential collision] the stranger settled his countenance stedfastly upon us, as if to search and value every element in the conflict before him. For five seconds more of his seventy he sat immovably, like one that mused on some great purpose. For five more. . . . (1896, 13:315)

What follows is a detailed account of the precise motions of the carriage in relation to the mail-coach. All told, it takes over a page to describe the final seconds before the crisis, the description ending with an extraordinary metaphor that describes the narrow miss: "Light does not tread upon the steps of light more indivisibly than did our all-conquering arrival upon the escaping efforts of the gig" (1896, 13:316).

The mail-coach is thus a device for producing sensuous and temporal disorientations that mirror the effects of opium. An analogous "machine" of disorientation for the juvenile De Quincey who had never taken opium was the "humming-top." As a child De Quincey was fascinated with the idea of an antigravity "humming-top" that, because of its "vertiginous motion" (1896, 1:64), would allow his brother to walk on the ceiling like a housefly. Certainly this fascination with such a fabulous device was merely childish fancy, but the impetus for the older De Quincey's description of the machine is his deep-seated predilection for extraordinary perception. Like the mail-coach, the humming-top alters the senses and induces a radical view of the world.

The psychological and sensual disorientation described in De Quincey's autobiographical writings and visionary prose is established through perceptual frames, objects and mechanisms, and physical journeys whose landscapes are determined by the psychologically and socially disorienting properties of opium. Accordingly, De Quincey's nursery experiences are not recollected in tranquility but come to him in "tempestuous uproars." His life journey, from its very beginning, is punctuated by a series of critical visionary events which determine its course and for which he will always bear a guilty conscience. Although these events in his autobiographical writings are structurally similar to the Wordsworthian "spots of time," De Quincey's moments—as he pauses over his sister's corpse, dreams in the church, leaves the Manchester Grammar School, or spends a turbulent night in the Shrewsbury hotel—are analogues of intoxication which deny all possibility of return to the Wordsworthian state of primal sympathy.

Three
Poe and the French Symbolists: Disjoining the Cultural Episteme

With Midnight to the North of Her—
And Midnight to the South of Her—
And Maelstrom—in the Sky—
  —Emily Dickinson, "Before me—dips Eternity"

De Quincey's stature in the history of postromantic letters is ambiguous and his place often camouflaged. Though his *Confessions* quickly became a literary sensation, his esoteric subject matter was not broadly emulated within the Christian mainstream of the Western tradition. The confessional literature of the Victorian era, with the emergence of figures like Newman and Mill, turned toward spiritual autobiography that generally reflected a reaffirmation of traditional values. Despite this trend, De Quincey became something of a writer's writer, significantly instructing the odd poet or fiction writer who recognized him as an original thinker and master prose stylist. In America, E. A. Poe praised De Quincey's then anonymous *Confessions* as "fine—very fine!—glorious imagination—deep philosophy—acute speculation—plenty of fire and fury, and a good spicing of the decidedly unintelligible" (Hayter 149). And in France Baudelaire acknowledged De Quincey's "infallibility" as *the* literary authority on opium, paying deference to the opium-eater by translating De Quincey's work rather than writing his own on the pleasures and pains of opium. Though De Quincey's impact on later romantic and symbolist writers is clear, I do not intend to demonstrate the obvious chronological influence of De Quincey on Poe, of Poe on Baudelaire, and of Baudelaire on Rimbaud. Rather, I shall explore how the ideas and methods of each writer grew out of De Quincey's seminal work. For the literary theories and practices of Baudelaire, Poe, and Rimbaud are based upon a common rejection of cultural perception, expressed by the outcast's estrangement from his homeland.

Baudelaire and the Theory of Correspondances

The common ground of De Quincey and Baudelaire is apparent in their mutual exploration of the effect of artificial stimulants on the literary imagination. Yet the moral conclusions that Baudelaire reaches regarding the use of wine, hashish, and opium differ from those of his predecessor. Though De Quincey is frank and graphic in his depiction of the pains of opium, and though one of his admirable qualities is the gift of unflinching introspection, the *Confessions* finally is an elaborate, subtle rationale for the author's addiction. He sidesteps moral issues and instead rationalizes his laudanum habit, citing his sensitivity, his precocity, or his grief and suffering as causes of his addiction. Baudelaire's perspective is more complex and even contradictory. A bohemian debauchee with a strong Catholic strain in his meditative letters and writing,[1] Baudelaire does not hesitate to address moral issues or to admonish his readers. Baudelaire also differs from De Quincey in his response to different kinds of intoxicants. Unlike De Quincey, who assails the intoxicating properties of wine,[2] Baudelaire celebrates the *"profondes joies du vin"* (304) and cautions against hashish intoxication, which he views as an essentially solipsistic activity. While both wine and hashish *"exaltent [la] personnalité"* (312), hashish is *"antisocial"* whereas *"la vin est profondément humain"* (308), or promotes a sense of fellow feeling among drinking companions. In his 1851 essay *"Du vin et du hachish,"* Baudelaire's most urgent warning is that hashish attacks the will, our most precious "organ":

> Enfin le vin est pour le peuple qui travaille et qui mérite d'en boire. Le hachish appartient à la classe des joies solitaires; il est fait pour les misérables oisifs. Le vin est utile, il produit des résultats fructifiants. Le hachish est inutile et dangereux. (312)

[Finally, wine is for the common people who work and who deserve to drink it. Hashish belongs to the class of solitary joys; it is made for lazy idlers. Wine is useful: it produces fruitful results. Hashish is useless and dangerous.]

By the end of the decade Baudelaire had grown more extreme in his attitude toward drugs that alter human consciousness. In *"Le Poëme du Haschisch"* (1860) Baudelaire's tone is more somber and admonishing (Mickel). Warning of hashish's capacity to diminish the will and creativity, Baudelaire writes without hesitation of *"le caractère immoral du haschisch"* and likens its habitual use to *"un suicide lent"* (583). For Baudelaire, drug taking becomes not only immoral and self-destructive, it becomes sinful.

Despite Baudelaire's expressed reservations about De Quincey and opium- or hashish-eating, he demonstrates great sympathy for the English prose writer. De Quincey's claim that the opium-eater is one divorced from his fellow man by a self-imposed liberation and exile is reiterated in Baudelaire's description of the opium-eater's relation to society at large:

> Ils s'écartent de la population commune, comme s'ils abdiquaient humblement tout droit à la camaraderie avec la grande famille humaine . . . cette nation contemplative perdue au sein de la nation active. (585)

> [They deviate from the common population as if they were humbly abdicating all right to camaraderie with the great family of man . . . this contemplative nation lost in the bosom of the active nation.]

This qualified sympathy, born out of Baudelaire's own consumption of opium and hashish, is corroborated by his sensitive inclusion of the most poignant sections of the *Confessions* in his translation of that work. In *Un Mangeur D'Opium*, Baudelaire does not chide De Quincey's excesses but instead emphasizes themes that preoccupied De Quincey: the pariah (1896, 3:122ff.), the London prostitute Ann and the tyranny of London faces (1896, 3:108), the nature of the opium vision (1896,

3:130ff.), and, most importantly, the sense of grief, suffering, and guilt that pervades the English author's work.

But since *Un Mangeur D'Opium* is really a condensation and selective translation of the *Confessions,* a method of writing called *rifacimento* used by De Quincey himself,[3] Baudelaire's work demonstrates experiential similarities and temperamental sympathies with De Quincey. Indeed, Baudelaire extended De Quincey's preoccupations. Though De Quincey was fascinated with the idea of using dreams in imaginative literature, he never really articulated a formal literary doctrine based on extraordinary sense perception as Baudelaire did. If Baudelaire was less pioneering than his English predecessor, his experimentation with states of heightened sense experience, specifically hyperesthesia and the genuine synesthesia encountered during hashish taking, led to an articulated and applicable aesthetic: the poetic theory of *correspondances.*

The hashish-inspired hyperesthesia recounted by Baudelaire in *"Le Poëme du Haschisch"* is not essentially different from that described by De Quincey. What Baudelaire and his associates in the *Club des hachischins* experienced is described as *"une acuité supérieure dans tous les sens"* (575). The main difference between the opium- and hashish-inspired sense experience is that while both increase the vividness of sense impressions, hashish is more likely to involve more of the senses and to engage them simultaneously (Hayter 152). The hashish user is more likely to experience genuine synesthesia, in which one sense stimulates or is confounded with another. Baudelaire describes the effects of hashish as a gradual intensification of sense impressions until all the senses are engaged in sympathetic stimulation:

> L'odorat, la vue, l'ouïe, le toucher participent également à ce progrès. Les yeux visent l'infini. L'oreille perçoit des sons presque insaisissables au milieu du plus vaste tumulte. C'est alors que commencent les hallucinations. Les objets extérieurs prennent lentement, successivement, des apparences singulières; ils se déforment et se transforment. Puis arrivent les équivoques, les méprises

et les transpositions d'idées. Les sons se revêtent de couleurs, et les couleurs contiennent une musique. (575)

[The senses of smell, sight, hearing, and touch participate equally in this development. The eyes aim towards infinity. The ears hear almost imperceptible sounds in the midst of the greatest tumult. It is then that hallucinations begin. One by one, external objects slowly take on extraordinary appearances. They deform and transform themselves. Next, ambiguities, misjudgments, and transposition of ideas occur. Sounds are endowed with color and colors contain a melody.]

According to Baudelaire's theory of *correspondances,* in part derived from the mysticism of Swedenborg (579) and in part an outgrowth of his Wagnerian criticism (Lehmann 207), any individual tone, sound, color, smell, or feeling has an analogue or equivalent in any other sensory category:

Correspondances

La Nature est un temple où de vivants piliers
Laissent parfois sortir de confuses paroles;
L'homme y passe à travers des forêts de symboles
Qui l'observent avec des regards familiers.

Comme de longs échos qui de loin se confondent
Dans une ténébreuse et profonde unité
Vaste comme la nuit et comme la clarté,
Les parfums, les couleurs et les sons se répondent.

Il est des parfums frais comme des chairs d'enfants,
Doux comme les hautbois, verts comme les prairies,
—Et d'autres, corrompus, riches et triomphants,

Ayant l'expansion des choses infinies,
Comme l'ambre, le musc, le benjoin, et l'encens,
Qui chantent les transports de l'esprit et des sens. (46)

[Nature is a temple where living pillars sometimes give out confused speech; there, man traverses forests of symbols, which observe him with familiar glances

> Like the long echoes that in the distance are medleyed in a dark and profound unity vast as the night and day, perfumes, colors, and sounds answer each other.
>
> There are perfumes cool as children's flesh, sweet as oboes, green as meadows, and others corrupt, rich and triumphant,
>
> Having the expanse of infinite things, like amber, musk, benjamin, and incense, which sing the transports of the spirit and the senses.]

Although the confluence of sensation is specific and real for Baudelaire the hashish-eater, the theory of *correspondances* is an imaginative construct that reflects a conscious literary epistemology in which the aim of the poet is to examine the interrelation of sense impressions that function as interpretable symbols. When the correspondences are identified, or in a sense created, as a metaphor might be created, the poet has conceived a profound unity among all things. Heightened sense perception brings the poet in contact with objects (symbols) that are not only individually expressive but that contribute to a choir of sights, sounds, colors, and odors which together express transcendent correspondences. This phenomenon is a direct descendent of the protosymbolist involutes of both Coleridge and De Quincey, whose symbolic complexes of image and emotion express truths that transcend ordinary perception.

Correspondances thus involve a mystical disjoining of the cultural episteme when the normal association between a sense perception and thought is subverted by the poet. In Baudelaire's work, this subversion frequently happens during a voyage of estrangement in which the poet-voyager imaginatively departs from the landscape of his culture. The voyage, in effect, becomes the counterpart of the opium dream. In his prose poem "L'Invitation au Voyage," Baudelaire explicitly correlates the journey away from one's native country with the opium dream, *"un vrai pays de Cocagne"*:

> Des rêves! toujours des rêves! et plus l'âme est ambitieuse et délicate, plus les rêves s'éloignent du possible.

> Chaque homme porte en lui sa dose d'opium naturel, incessamment sécrétée et renouvelée. (159)
>
> [Dreams, forever dreams! The more the soul is ambitious and delicate, the more do dreams get away from the possible. Each man has in himself his dose of natural opium, incessantly secreted and renewed.]

For Baudelaire the voyage becomes a conventionalized metaphor for estrangement from cultural experience and perception. In two centerpieces of his poetic canon, "L'Invitation au Voyage" and "Le Voyage," Baudelaire explores opposing states of mind that elicit the pleasures and pains of departing from one's native land. In the former work, the journey is toward a state of ideal love—toward *"[le] pays qui te ressemble!"*—an imaginative country which resembles the love itself, where *"tout n'est qu'ordre et beauté, / Luxe, calme, et volupté"* (72). Later, in the voyage the poet's speaker, still searching for new lands, laments: *"Amer savoir, celui qu'on tire du voyage!"* (124). The voyage results in a bitter knowledge, for the journey is toward death:

> O Mort, vieux capitaine, il est temps! levons l'ancre!
> Ce pays nous ennuie, ô Mort! Appareillons!
> Si le ciel et la mer sont noirs comme de l'encre,
> Nos co eurs que tu connais sont remplis de rayons!
>
> Verse-nous ton poison pour qu'il nous réconforte!
> Nous voulons, tant ce feu nous brûle le cerveau,
> Plonger au fond du gouffre, Enfer ou Ciel, qu'importe?
> Au fond de l'Inconnu pour trouver du *nouveau!* (124)
>
> [O Death, old captain, it is time! Pull up the anchor! This country tires us, O Death! Let us get under way! If the sky and the sea are black as ink, our hearts, as you know, are full of light!
>
> Pour us your poison to comfort us! So much this fire is burning our minds, we want to plunge to the bottom of the abyss—hell or heaven, what does it matter—into the depths of the Unknown in order to find something *new!*]

In both poems the journey itself corresponds to an imaginative state and, as such, becomes a kind of perception. The disjoining of the cultural episteme thus occurs on the imagistic as well as the metaphorical level. Image, figure (symbol), and theme are one.

Poe and the Disjoining of Cultural Value

Baudelaire's interest in heightened states of sense perception and the synesthetic correspondences of sense experiences is derived as much from Poe as from De Quincey (Tate 241n). Like De Quincey, Poe found the imagery of intoxication an expressive means for describing the visionary faculty and the literary imagination. The convention of intoxication in Poe's tales is analogous to heightened sensibility that is variously expressed in hyperesthesia, synesthesia, and the sensation of vertigo or entropy. This fascination with extraordinary sense perception is compounded with what D. H. Lawrence has identified as Poe's intense concern with "the disintegration-processes of his own psyche" (65). In Poe's tales the reader participates in a systematic stripping away of conventional perception that leads to a state of physical, psychical, or allegorical collapse.

Poe's work generally displays a preoccupation with heightened sense perception or the mortal disintegration of the body. In his tales of the sea, these two preoccupations frequently merge and form allegories of epistemological disintegration. As the journeyer casts off from his cultural moorings, he is confronted with a totally new visual and kinesthetic reality and is forced to question all he was once sure of. Works such as "A Descent into the Maelström," "MS. Found in a Bottle," and *The Narrative of Arthur Gordon Pym of Nantucket,* whether they describe circular or linear voyages, are thus descendents of Coleridge's "Rime of the Ancient Mariner." Each of Poe's tales describes a mariner's voyage away from the familiar and his discovery of another level of consciousness or realm of being.

"A Descent into the Maelström" offers an archetypal journey of death and rebirth largely consistent with the Christian episteme. Though the tale teller enters a kind of heretical space, he returns to the embrace of his culture. The tale is told to an unnamed auditor-narrator who listens to the story on a craggy mountain peak which offers a vertiginous outlook over the Norwegian "Moskoe-ström":

> the vast bed of the waters, seamed and scarred into a thousand conflicting channels, burst suddenly into phrensied convulsion—heaving boiling, hissing—gyrating in gigantic and innumerable vortices, and all whirling and plunging on to the eastward with a rapidity which water never elsewhere assumes except in precipitous descents. (Poe 1978, 2:580)

From several miles away, the old fisherman and the narrator watch as the maelstrom forms a "terrific funnel... speeding dizzily round and round with a swaying and sweltering motion" (2:580). Poe has chosen his setting carefully, for the distant perspective emphasizes the importance of sense perception in the tale, and the disorienting entry into heretical space is consistent with the landscapes of Coleridge and De Quincey. The old fisherman describes, in hyperesthetic terms, the vertiginous sensation of being caught in and dragged down by the maelstrom; he is "enveloped in foam," feels the "amazing velocity" of the boat, and skims "like an air bubble up on the surface of the surge" which appears as a "huge writhing wall" (2:588). During the gradual whirling descent, the old man experiences periods of "stupor" (586), "confusion of mind occasioned by the wind and spray together" (589), light-headedness, and even delirium (591). The effect is a sustained synesthesia. But clearly these overlapping sensations have none of the mystical properties of Baudelaire's *correspondances;* rather, this state of sensate confusion marks the moment of death, or the verge of sleep (Wilbur 257), or some other kind of consciousness beyond normal waking experience. Whatever the symbolic significance of the journey, the returning fisherman completes a Christian circuit and expresses no deep estrangement from his culture.

Poe's earlier tale, "MS. Found in a Bottle," describes the same phenomenon of the maelstrom but offers a narrative structure that subverts the death-rebirth archetype. Coleridge's Ancient Mariner here comes more clearly to mind due to the "estrangement" of the narrator from his native land and his journey "farther to the southward than any previous navigators" (2:139). Moreover, the tale offers no circular return, no apparent rebirth; the narrator lives on only through his anonymous manuscript which closes with a series of disjointed impressions. The first of these discrete meditations defines the importance of the writer's extraordinary sense perceptions but at the same time asserts that they are ineffable:

> A feeling, for which I have no name, has taken possession of my soul—a sensation which will admit of no analysis, to which the lessons of by-gone time are inadequate, and for which I fear futurity itself will offer me no key. To a mind constituted like my own, the latter consideration is an evil. I shall never—I know that I shall never—be satisfied with regard to the nature of my conceptions. Yet it is not wonderful that these conceptions are indefinite, since they have their origin in sources so utterly novel. A new sense—a new entity is added to my soul. (2:141)

The narrator finds that his previous experience at sea fails to prepare him for his voyage aboard the DISCOVERY. The cultural codes of language and sensation and the analysis of lessons of the past are inadequate to his present experience. At first sight of the ship, the writer feels "an indefinite sense of awe" (2:140). He finds the hoary, spectral crew members who ignore him are "incomprehensible men!" (2:141), and the construction of the ship itself is "of a material to which [he is] a stranger" (2:142). He regards the captain with "a feeling of irrepressible reverence and awe mingled with the sensation of wonder" (2:144). In short, his journey aboard the DISCOVERY severs him from his comfortable sense of reality and takes him into a heretical space. Once he boards the DISCOVERY, he is inevitably drawn into a vortex of the incomprehensible. His sensations defy description; his place in time and space is obscure.

The experimental narrative of the tale reflects this incomprehensibility. Once inside heretical space, the writer-narrator apparently ceases to exist among the company of specters; he is himself imperceptible. His narration mirrors this epistemological shift, breaking down into a series of discrete, disjointed diary entries which reflect, on a linguistic level, the disruption of sequential experience and certain knowledge. Time, in effect, ceases to exist. Sensations, too, cease: "All in the immediate vicinity of the ship is the blackness of eternal night, and a chaos of foamless water . . . looking like the walls of the universe" (2:145). And the universe disintegrates:

> Oh, horror upon horror!—the ice opens suddenly to the right, and to the left, and we are whirling dizzily, in immense concentric circles, round and round the borders of a gigantic amphitheatre, the summit of whose walls is lost in the darkness and the distance. But little time will be left me to ponder upon my destiny! The circles rapidly grow small—we are plunging madly within the grasp of the whirlpool—and amid a roaring, and bellowing, and thundering of ocean and of tempest, the ship is quivering—oh God! and—going down! (2:146)

Poe's allegory can be read on several levels, but clearly in one sense the journey is a descent into another realm of consciousness, into a heretical universe from which there is no return. The final plunge is not compensated by a miraculous ascent, as in "A Descent into the Maelström." Only the manuscript itself returns to civilization.

Estrangement from the cultural episteme is also the dominant theme of *The Narrative of Arthur Gordon Pym of Nantucket*. As in the earlier tales, Poe's novel is structured by a series of deaths and rebirths—Pym's enclosure in the box, his disguise as the corpse of Rogers, his archetypal becalming and reanimation, his live burial and emergence from the cave-in—

all of which take place on a voyage that parallels the Ancient Mariner's. Pym journeys toward the South Pole, is visited by an albatross and a death ship, and encounters a land where everything is unknown. Like the experience of Poe's earlier characters in "A Descent into the Maelström" and "MS. Found in a Bottle," Pym's allegorical death and rebirth is accompanied by psychic disturbance and heightened states of perception. The most notable instance is Pym's "disorder of mind" when he becomes sick and is enclosed in the box. His dreams and visions in the darkness are, like the "perturbed sleep occasioned by opium" (73), filled with hyperesthetic images that make his senses supersensitive when he awakes. The sensate extremes of the later sea chapters—the storm, the "dead calm" afterwards, and the gradual disintegration of the *Grampus*—are structural analogues of Pym's individual death and rebirth. The Christian archetype of death and rebirth, however, is subverted by dramatic sequences that contribute to the motif of estrangement from culture.

The first events of the novel begin to develop this theme. The mutiny that occurs aboard the *Grampus* is a figurative dissolution of civilization, underscored by the unusually brutal murder of Captain Bernard and over twenty crewmen loyal to the order that the Captain represents. Poe describes the "horrible butchery" (84) in explicit detail not only to emphasize the degree to which cultural values are betrayed but to foreshadow subsequent events in the novel. While Pym and his friend Augustus (the captain's son) are horrified by the mutiny, they later reenact the butchery in their cannibalism. Here, too, the event profoundly distances the men from cultural values; Pym finds himself rendered helpless by an "abject and pitiable terror" of consuming human flesh. Filled with a "diabolical hatred," he falls into a swoon only to wake to the murder of Parker (144–46) whose remains the surviving crew members consume over a four-day period. Pym's loss of consciousness before partaking of human flesh is a psychical threshold that, like the ancient Mariner's swoon, marks the boundary between the culturally sanctioned and the forbidden. Once this Rubicon is crossed, Pym and his surviving companions are literally and allegorically estranged from culture. "The Rime of the Ancient Mariner" provides an interesting contrast with Poe's novel. The marriage feast from which the Mariner is excluded is a symbol of cultural continuity; whereas in Poe's narrative the mutiny and cannibalism in which Pym and his companions are unwilling participants are symbols of cultural dissolution. During the mutiny, social order is disrupted as the authority relationships are broken down. During the act of cannibalism, individuals are dismembered and their flesh consumed: Augustus's arm putrefies and, after his death, his "entire leg came off in [Peters's] grasp" (155).

The final sequence of events in the novel, Pym's sojourn among the south Atlantic islanders, is, like other major sections, introduced by detailed, elaborate digression. Rivalling De Quincey in this art, Poe uses the digressions on navigation, the history of exploration, and ornithology as a means of severing the reader from his or her own sense of fictive reality. It is through the art of digression that the reader is led from the "facts" of the narration into the world of the unknown.[4] When Pym and his new companions from the *Jane Guy* disembark to explore the south Atlantic islands, the reader is thus prepared for an unknown realm: "At every step we took inland the conviction forced itself upon us that we were in a country differing essentially from any hitherto visited by civilized men. We saw nothing with which we had had been formerly conversant" (193). In keeping with the travel literature of his time, Poe is simply making his tale as attractively exotic as he could, and yet the physical setting and geography are soon transformed. When Pym in buried alive by a cave-in orchestrated by the seemingly harmless islanders, the merely exotic journey assumes a cosmic significance:

> I was suddenly aware of a concussion resembling nothing I had ever before experienced, and which impressed me with a vague conception, if indeed I then thought of

> anything, that the whole foundations of the solid globe were suddenly rent asunder, and that the day of universal dissolution was at hand. (207)

While one senses a certain ironic detachment in Poe's description, the exaggeration is in keeping with the images in "A Descent" and "MS." which end in the dissolution of the universe. And, in a sense, that is what happens to Pym and Dirk Peters; the known world collapses around them, they are separated from members of their culture, and they are all left for dead by the island inhabitants. Although Pym escapes entombment and eventually the islands themselves, his life and the novel end tumultuously, with Pym's homeward-bound vessel plunging "into the embraces of the cataract" during a storm at sea.

The ending of *Pym* is also in keeping with that of "The Fall of the House of Usher" which, more than any of Poe's tales, is an allegory of the disjoining of the cultural episteme. This interpretation, while not definitive, is consistent with other persuasive readings that focus on the notion of psychic collapse. Clearly, Poe's central concern in the tale is with epistemological questions.[5] The narrator's description of the physiognomy of the house with its "vacant eye-like windows" (Poe 1978, 2:397) and the sensation it evokes—"an utter depression of soul which I can compare to no earthly sensation more properly than to the after-dream of the reveller upon opium" (2:397)—indicate Poe's preoccupation with human perception as a theme in the story. Of course Poe is not interested in common, everyday perception but the heightened sensibilities of the Usher race, who practice the highest forms of art and social benevolence:

> His very ancient family had been noted, time out of mind, for a peculiar sensibility of temperament, displaying itself, through long ages, in many works of exalted art, and manifested, of late, in repeated deeds of munificent yet unobtrusive charity, as well as in a passionate devotion to the intricacies, perhaps even more than to the orthodox and easily recognisable beauties, of musical science. (2:398–99)

Roderick Usher, a member of the highest social order, is an accomplished musician, abstract painter, poet, theosopher, and man of letters. A refined practitioner of the most subtle arts of his culture, Usher falls victim to his training and aristocratic pedigree which have afflicted him with a nervous disorder.

The refined Usher sensibility ironically burdens him with a "morbid acuteness of the senses" (2:403) so that all tastes, odors, sights, and sounds are oppressive. His clinical hyperesthesia and wide reading in mysticism give rise to an animistic world view in which all vegetable things are sentient:

> In his disordered fancy [about the sentience of vegetable things], the idea had assumed a more daring character, and trespassed, under certain conditions, upon the kingdom of inorganization. . . . This belief, however, was connected (as I have previously hinted) with the gray stones of the home of his forefathers. The conditions of the sentience had been here, he imagined, fulfilled in the method of collocation of these stones—in the order of their arrangement, as well as in that of the many *fungi* which overspread them, and of the decayed trees which stood around. (2:408)

Usher performs a transfusion of sense experience, tapping his own superabundance of sensation to endow the inanimate (inorganized) world with life, or sensation. His faculties invest the House of Usher with a spiritual intellect felt by the narrator as he approaches the estate. In a sense, Roderick Usher and the House of Usher are one. And since Usher represents the highest achievements of our civilization, when he collapses and the house itself disintegrates, so does our civilization. Poe's tale suggests that Usher's psychic disintegration is an allegory for the disintegration of cultural knowledge and value.

Rimbaud's Dérèglement de Tous les Sens

Whereas Roderick Usher and the narrator of his story are unwilling participants in the disintegration of the psyche and the cultural episteme, Arthur Rimbaud, the literary descendent of both Poe and Baudelaire, considers this process crucial to the liberation of the literary imagination. Rimbaud's poetic theories and his poetry have much in common with De Quincey, Poe, and Baudelaire, for all were interested in the effect of artificial stimulants on the functioning of the imagination. Baudelaire's theory of *correspondances* had an unequivocal impact on Rimbaud, whose often quoted letters on the *voyant* praise Baudelaire as *"le premier voyant, roi de poètes,* un vrai Dieu" (Lettres 68). This youthful apotheosis led to some interesting but derivative experiments such as *"Voyelles,"* which is based on Baudelaire's doctrine of *correspondances*. For Rimbaud, *correspondances* were a celebration of sense experience and a means of transcending ordinary perception to experience the mystical, universal connection among all things. But just as Baudelaire came to distance himself from De Quincey, Rimbaud finally rejected Baudelaire. The means by which Rimbaud pursued his own vision were in direct conflict with Baudelaire's admonitions in *"Du vin et du hachish"* and *Le Poëme du Haschisch."*

In his 13 May 1871 letter to Isambard, Rimbaud expresses a literary epistemology based on his personal experiments with altered states of awareness. During this period, Rimbaud would deliberately fatigue himself and then take large quantities of coffee, tobacco, and wine in various combinations (Rickword 48): *"Maintenant, je m'encrapule le plus possible. Pourquoi? Je veux être poète, et je travaille à me rendre* voyant: *vous ne comprendez pas du tout, et je ne saurais presque vous expliquer. Il s'agit d'arriver à l'inconnu par le dérèglement de* tous les sens" (Rimbaud 1931, 55). [Right now I'm debauching myself as much as possible. Why? I want to be a poet, and I am working at making myself a *visionary:* you will not understand all of it, and I'm not sure if I can explain it to you. It is a question of arriving at the unknown by a derangement of *all the senses.*] Two days after writing this letter, Rimbaud sent his famous letter to Demeny in which he speaks of the same issues with more specificity and authority:

> Le Poète se fait *voyant* par un long, immense et raisonné *dérèglement* de *tous les sens*. Toutes les formes d'amour, de souffrance, de folie; il cherche lui-même, il épuise en lui tous les poisons pour n'en garder que les quintessences. Ineffable torture où il a besoin de toute la foi, de toute la force surhumaine, où il devient entre tous le grand malade, le grand criminel, le grand maudit,—et le suprême Savant!—Car, il arrive à l'*inconnu!* (62)
>
> [The poet makes himself a *visionary* by a long, immense and reasoned *derangement* of *all the senses*. All forms of love, suffering, and madness; he looks into himself, he exhausts in himself all poisons in order to keep only their quintessences. Ineffable torture where he needs all the faith, all the superhuman strength in the world, where he becomes, among all, the great invalid, the great criminal, the great outcast—and the supreme Scientist—Because, he arrives at the *unknown!*]

What a few days before had been a rather hesitant claim to becoming a visionary poet is here transformed into an articulate, daring abnegation of sobriety and traditional social value. In order to become a *voyant,* Rimbaud declares the poet must undergo a radical, systematic derangement of the senses, a violent process that Hart Crane called "rapturous and explosive destructivism" (231) and that, more recently, has been described as "deconstructing the self" into a "scattered or disseminated self" (Bersani x–xi).

In order to dis-integrate the socially approved self, the poet must undermine social convention, a process that divests the self of cultural competence. The deconstruction of the socially structured self occurs through a systematic negating of the culturally accepted associations among sense experience, knowledge, and value. Such a dissolution of the social self through a *"dérèglement de tous les sens"* is apparent in the opening lines of *"Le Bateau ivre":*

> Comme je descendais des Fleuves impassibles,
> Je ne me sentis plus guidé par les haleurs:

Des Peaux-Rouges criards les avaient pris pour cibles,
Les ayant cloués nus aux poteaux de couleurs.

J'étais insoucieux de tous les équipages,
Porteur de blés flamands ou de cotons anglais.
Quand avec mes haleurs ont fini ces tapages,
Les Fleuves m'ont laissé descendre où je voulais.
(Rimbaud 1966, 114)

[As I drifted down impassible rivers, I no longer felt myself guided by haulers: loud red-skins had made targets of them, having nailed them naked to colored stakes.

I cared nothing for any boats, carrying Flemish wheat or English cotton. When the uproar was done with my haulers, the River left me drift where I wanted.]

As the *"haleurs"* relinquish control of the boat and the *voyant* feels his lack of guidance, he responds to the world with absolute freedom, shedding the restraints imposed by family, fellow humans, and the daily commerce of the world. Drifting carelessly and aimlessly down the river, the *voyant* imagines a coalescence of the sea, the poem, and the vision. The visionary poet immerses himself in the natural sensate world, and the boundary between self and the purifying elemental world is dissolved:

Et dès lors, je me suis baigné dans le Poème
De la Mer, infusé d'astres, et lactescent,
Dévorant les azurs verts; où flottaison blême
Et ravie, un noyé pensif parfois descend;

Où, teignant tout à coup les bleuités, délires
Et rhythmes lents sous les rutilements du jour,
Plus fortes que l'alcool, plus vastes que nos lyres,
Fermentent les rousseurs amères de l'amour! (116)

[And from then on, I bathed in the Poem of the Sea, infused with stars and swirling milk, devouring the green azures; where, pale and entranced flotsam, a passive drowned man sometimes drifts by;

Where, suddenly tinting the blueness, deliriums and slow rhythms under the glowing of day, stronger than spirits, vaster than our lyres, ferments the bitter redness of love!)

The *"Poème de la Mer"* is a synesthetic tumult of images, described by Rimbaud's friend Delahaye as a "precipitous flow of violent sensations" (Rickword 33). The catalogue of images and sense impressions reflect the actual process of disjoining the cultural episteme; that is, the dissolution of conventional perception and its replacement with a new self and a new world created by the *voyant*. The poet feels himself *"jeté par l'ouragan dans l'éther sans oiseau,"* [thrown by the hurricane into the birdless sphere], now a *"bateau perdu"* drifting dead-drunk and free through a universe he himself creates. Rimbaud carries the romantic-symbolist epistemology to an extreme, projecting a heretical cosmogeny in which the myth-making poet is the center of a universe that wheels vertiginously around him. And yet, as Henry Miller argues, Rimbaud is no "madman whirling about the pivot of self" (87). He is "concerned with the problem of the soul, with the expansion of consciousness and the creation of new moral values. [He is] at the hub of [a] wheel which sheds light on the void" (112). Like his romantic predecessors, Coleridge and De Quincey, Rimbaud engages in a heretical epistemology that is simultaneously destructive and constructive, fragmenting the old and projecting the new.

"Le Bateau ivre" ends with a final renunciation. Delighting in the "ecstatic agony" of his voyage (Peschel 56), the *voyant* rejects any possibility of return to his native land:

> Je ne puis plus, baigné de vos langueurs, ô lames,
> Enlever leur sillage aux porteurs de cotons,
> Ni traverser l'orgueil des drapeaux et des flammes,
> Ni nager sous les yeux horribles des pontons. (Rimbaud 1966, 120)

> [I can no longer, bathed in your languors, o waves, sail in the wakes of the cotton boats, nor encounter the pride of flags and pennants, nor row under the horrible eyes of prisoner-ships.]

After his prolonged and willed derangement of the senses, the *voyant* has shed his social and moral responsibilities as well as his national and familial identity. Rimbaud's antipathy toward contemporary Christian European civilization led him to divest himself of its mode of perception. This desire starts, he writes in "Matinée d'ivresse," "*par quelques dégoûts et cela finit,—ne pouvant nous saisir sur-le-champ de cette éternité,—cela finit par une débandade de parfums*" (232). [(It starts) with a few disgusts and it ends—we cannot immediately seize this eternity—it ends in a confusion of perfumes.] The poet's determined renunciation of the cultural episteme begins with a disgust for oneself and all cultural modes of perception and, after a willed derangement of the senses, ends in a riot of perfumes.

Outlining the literary kinship of Rimbaud, De Quincey, Poe, and Baudelaire does more than establish a line of literary descent or influence; it defines a tradition that had a significant impact upon modern literature. In its most obvious manifestations, the tradition of these symbolist writers depends on a heretical departure from cultural sobriety. The resulting disorientation of the senses and spirit ends in a visionary estrangement from cultural perception. Although the sensory derangement described by the nineteenth-century writers in this tradition was drug-induced, the disorienting journey became a literary convention in that most heretical of periods, the modern age.

Four
The Nocturnal Visions of Joyce and Barnes

The experience of reality is an hermeneutic task. We can find, in a preliminary disorganization of the senses, the point of departure for the capture of the chthonian universe.
—Eugene Jolas, *The Language of Night*

When Sylvia Beach claims that Djuna Barnes was "one of the most fascinating literary figures in the Paris of the twenties" (112), we immediately recognize Joyce's implied presence in such a remark. Perhaps Beach was echoing Barnes's early assessment of Joyce's work, an assessment of journalistic restraint that belied the young novelist's enthusiasm for the fiction of her fellow exile. Shortly after the publication of *Ulysses*, Barnes complimented Joyce in her *Vanity Fair* article, "James Joyce," by subtitling the piece "A Portrait of the Man Who is, at Present, One of the More Significant Figures in Literature" (65). In private, however, when *Ulysses* was first published in *The Little Review*, Barnes remarked: "I shall never write another line. Who has the nerve to after this!" (Field 108). Luckily, Barnes did not heed her own call for novelists to abandon their writing, for if she had we would now be without what is arguably the single piece of modern fiction in English that rivals Joyce's exploration of the night world inhabited by characters estranged from their cultures.

In this exploration, Joyce and Barnes were less teacher and disciple than fellow writers working toward visions of a heretical night world. Their characters, along with the reader, experience sensual, linguistic, and social disorientation. What results may be termed a literature of estrangement in which characters

References to Joyce's *Ulysses* cite episode number and line reference [e.g. (12.237)], and references to *Finnegans Wake* cite page and line reference [e.g. (327.33–35)]. All other references to works by Joyce cite page number only.

who are operating on the fringe of society distort physical appearances, social manners, and customs in order to create an altered perception of reality in the reader. Both Joyce and Barnes choose a sexual motif for their stories of the night world, for it is in the procreative and sexual life that the adherent to culture fulfills his or her social destiny. Joyce's and Barnes's estranged characters are like the Ancient Mariner who is drawn to the communal experience of the wedding feast but unable to participate in it. Social deviants like Bloom, the new womanly man in *Ulysses* and the hermaphroditic Matthew O'Connor in *Nightwood* offer a disorienting and heretical view of the psyche.

Yet the night worlds of Joyce and Barnes are different. Paradoxically, Joyce uses the culture's body of literature to structure his Walpurgisnacht, while Barnes creates a night world that is sui generis. Although Barnes and Joyce are both highly allusive, only Joyce's text displays its cultural erudition as it disjoins the cultural episteme; Barnes's text forces the reader through a kind of unlearning process as her characters dispense with custom and everyday perception.

Joyce, Epiphany, and the Association of Sensibility

Joyce's interest in the night world and in metaphors that define modes of perceiving that world extends far back into his career, and those metaphors are drawn from the diverse and large baggage of literary history that Joyce toted with him. Joyce's nocturnal vision has historical roots in the medieval dream vision, but Joyce's interests were probably closer to home, in the mystical, romantic, and symbolist writers who deliberately exploited intoxication for formal purposes, celebrating sense disorientation as a means of achieving a more radical kind of epistemological and cultural disorientation symbolized by the night world. Joyce's personal and literary fascination with Rimbaud is of central importance in Joyce's literary development and his sense of place in literary history, for the poetic theories of Rimbaud inform Joyce's early work.[1] Oliver Gogarty (the model for Buck Mulligan) mentions in a number of printed sources that Joyce was so taken with Rimbaud as an artistic rebel and social outlaw that he imitated the poet in his manner of dress and in his attitude toward social and artistic convention. In 1950 Gogarty reminisced about this influence and emphatically stated that Joyce could be understood only in the context of Rimbaud's work and ideas:

> From Flushing I received a postcard with a photograph of Joyce dressed to resemble Arthur Rimbaud. Rimbaud's revolution against established canons made him a god to Joyce. We must not leave Rimbaud out of the reckoning; if we do we will fail to understand the influences that fashioned Joyce. Rimbaud, disgusted with mankind, had withdrawn from the world. The logical end was for him to withdraw from all authorship because his kind of private writing would lead only to talking to himself. Joyce did not withdraw, so he ended by listening to himself talking in his sleep—"Finnegans Wake." (9)

Just as Rimbaud revered Baudelaire as a divine figure, so Joyce celebrated Rimbaud as a literary god. Joyce's adoption of a Rimbaudian *"dérèglement de tous les sens"* can be seen throughout Joyce's canon.[2] In *Stephen Hero,* Stephen's rather stilted philosophical discussion with McCann ranges over the differences between natural and artificial stimulants, with Stephen attacking McCann's moral objections to intoxication. These notions on intoxication, or at least the sense disorientation associated with it, inform the aesthetic theories of *Stephen Hero,* and while these theories are substantially different than those of *Portrait of the Artist as a Young Man,* they provide the essential epistemological structure of the epiphanies in *Portrait.* This structure is anticipated in Stephen's early definition of epiphany: "Imagine my glimpses at that clock as the gropings of a spiritual eye which seeks to adjust its vision to an exact focus. The moment the focus is reached the object is epiphanised"

(Joyce 1944, 211). The key to Joyce's early aesthetics and epistemology is this movement from visual blur to visual acuity, or metaphorically, from sensual disorientation to intellectual or spiritual understanding. The process Stephen describes thus resembles what Eliot would later call an association of sensibility through which a physical sensation becomes a state of mind. Eliot's statement on literary epistemology, succinctly summarized in his short essay on the metaphysical poets, advocates "a mechanism of sensibility which [can] devour any kind of experience" (247). Donne, Eliot argued, felt his thoughts, while poets writing later in the century underwent a "dissociation of sensibility" after which they generally "thought and felt by fits" (248). What Eliot praises in the metaphysical poets was "a fidelity to thought and feeling" which could best be accomplished by "transmuting ideas into sensations" or, conversely, by "transforming an observation into a state of mind" (249). Joyce's early epistemology also suggests a traditional Aristotelian hierarchy of responses to the world—imperfect sensation leading to more perfect intellection—but it closes the gap between sensation, thought, and some kind of imaginative or spiritual awareness. In each chapter of *Portrait,* sensual derangement precedes or presages altered awareness and a rejection of cultural values or social customs.

In *Portrait* these moments of association of sensibility characteristically begin with a Rimbaudian *dérèglement de tous les sens* which often occurs in darkness. The pandying incident stems from visual disorientation and underscores the conflict between the perceiving individual and cultural authority. When Stephen challenges Father Dolan's action, his psychological turmoil is reflected in the image of the disorienting labyrinth of Dedalus:

> He had reached the door and, turning quickly up to the right, . . . entered the low dark narrow corridor that led to the castle. And as he crossed the threshold of the door of the corridor he saw . . . that all the fellows were looking after him as they went filing by.
>
> He passed along the narrow dark corridor, . . .

> peered in front of him and right and left through the gloom and thought that those must be portraits. It was dark and silent and his eyes were weak and tired with tears so that he could not see. (55)

Like Thomas De Quincey, who reports in *Suspiria de Profundis* that his visionary sense was "aided by a slight defect of the eyes,"[3] Joyce here closely associates the concept of epiphany, or sudden awareness, with the clouding of physiological vision. This intimate connection between sensual derangement that precedes the altered consciousness of self and the rejection of cultural authority again occurs in chapter 2 as Stephen wanders "by day and by night . . . among distorted images of the outer world" (99). This distortion intensifies as Stephen enters the night world of Dublin's red-light district:

> He had wandered into a maze of narrow and dirty streets. From the foul laneways he heard bursts of hoarse riot and wrangling and drawling of drunken singers. . . . Women and girls dressed in long vivid gowns traversed the street from house to house. They were leisurely and perfumed. A trembling seized him and his eyes grew dim. The yellow gasflames arose before his troubled vision against the vapoury sky, burning as if before an altar. Before the doors and in the lighted halls groups were gathered arrayed as for some rite. He was in another world: he had awakened from a slumber of centuries. (100)

When Stephen enters nighttown, the rite of passage he undergoes is more than one of sexual experience; it is a Rimbaudian withdrawal into "another world," a subculture that has rejected the values of the dominant culture. Stephen's dim eyesight and "troubled vision" precede an altered perception of himself, particularly in relation to cultural mores and sexual taboos.

Other epiphanies in *Portrait* are preceded by the imperfect focus described in *Stephen Hero*. After Father Arnell's sermon, Stephen contemplates his soul in a "region of viscid gloom," a darkness inhabited by fiends and lascivious "goatish creatures."

As Stephen prays, momentarily embracing a cultural value, he looks out upon the darkened night city enveloped in a "yellowish haze" as "his eyes [are] dimmed with tears" (136–39). The heretical reversal of this momentary embrace of the church again occurs at night in the bird-girl epiphany during which Stephen's eyelids "trembled as if they felt the strange light of some new world. His soul was swooning into some new world, fantastic, dim, uncertain as under sea, traversed by cloudy shapes and beings" (172). This famous passage, perhaps more than any other in the novel, displays the connection between sensual derangement, altered vision, and a rejection of the cultural episteme. The new world Stephen enters is one of "profane joy." The Latin sense of *pro fanum,* meaning "before (outside) the temple," would have occurred to Joyce. Outside the sacred temple of Irish culture, Stephen is neither moral nor sensual in his response. He does not deny the beauty of the girl by mortifying his senses, nor does he betray any of his former teenage lasciviousness. Seeking to become, in Cranly's words, "a heretic or an outlaw" (245), his response is aesthetic: he pares his fingernails.

In *Portrait,* Joyce thus uses the night world as a metaphor for heretical perception and estrangement from one's culture. And often, entry into the night world structurally anticipates visionary experience. In each chapter, there is a moment of sensate discontinuity that brings a new perception of reality which subverts cultural values. This discontinuous structure is purified and amplified in *Giacomo Joyce,* a text Joyce was writing during the final composing of *Portrait* and the early drafting of *Ulysses* (Ellmann xi). Rarely the subject of critical scrutiny, *Giacomo Joyce* offers us a clear illustration of how Joyce viewed the potential of a discontinuous structure similar to his collection of epiphanies. The love prose poem is a series of epiphanic occasions presented as discrete visual units. In this work, like the later "Wandering Rocks" episode of *Ulysses,* the normal reading process is subverted by the montage structure. The reader pauses between isolated literary units that are separated by varying amounts of blank space. Narrative structure is imposed by the associative imagination of the reader, who is forced to make imaginative connections traditionally supplied by the narrator or author. *Giacomo Joyce* is, to use Barthes's terms, a "text of bliss" in which the reading process, anything but easy, requires the reader to reestablish continually his or her orientation to the text. This disorienting structure would become a standard literary technique in Joyce's later fiction.

Joyce's experimentation with a discontinuous structure in both *Portrait* and *Giacomo Joyce* provided him with a firm sense of how to structure individual passages and the overall structure of his next novel, *Ulysses*. The texture of individual episodes or passages in *Ulysses* is similar to that of *Giacomo Joyce*, and the structure of the entire novel mirrors a single chapter of *Portrait*. "Circe" and "Penelope" may be thought of as episodic epiphanies, or, rather, the night world in "Circe" depicts sensate derangement that anticipates the epiphany in "Penelope." In either case, the form of sense derangement associated with hallucination or hypnagogic monologue is laid out in "Proteus" when Stephen takes his epistemological ramble on Sandymount.

In *Ulysses*, as in *Portrait*, we see Stephen preoccupied with the relation of sensation to thought. On Sandymount strand, not far from the setting of his final epiphany in *Portrait*, Stephen experiments with an association of sensibility:[4] "Ineluctable modality of the visible," he intones to himself, "at least that if no more, thought through my eyes. Signatures of all things I am here to read" (3.1–2). Stephen's thought through his eyes and his inversion "shut your eyes and see" (3.9) are epistemological experiments that anticipate the extended sense disorientation of "Circe," an episode that functions structurally much like the moments of sensual disorientation of *Portrait*. But the main activity of the episode is an intellectual cataloguing of the various epistemological problems of Western civilization as posed by Aristotle, Berkeley, Jacob Boehme, and others. Paradoxically, Stephen is thus an intellectual embodiment of the cultural episteme he seeks to deny or transcend. He knows what our culture knows and is even vain about his learning, but at the same time he is dissatisfied with perpetuating that knowledge in a bookish way. He accordingly abandons his role of teacher in "Nestor" and seeks to subvert that cultural identity in "Circe" through drunkenness, disorientation, and immoral activity.

The appropriate literary technique for "Circe" is thus hallucination, a technique initiated by Bloom's entry as he passes before concave and convex mirrors: *"A concave mirror at the side presents to him lovelorn longlost lugubru Booloohoom. Grave Gladstone sees him level, Bloom for Bloom. He passes, struck by the stare of truculent Wellington, but in the convex mirror grin unstruck the bonham eyes and fatchuck cheekchops of Jollypoldy the rixdix doldy"* (15.145–49). The sense distortion and disorientation not only initiates the chaotic nocturnal vision of nighttown, but it anticipates the transformations through which Bloom will pass. This night landscape, perceived with distorted vision, is a product of what Eugene Jolas has termed the "language of night," a vocabulary explored by Rimbaud who first "envisaged 'the hallucination of words'" (19) that Joyce adapted in *Ulysses* as he "disintegrat[ed] words" (30). This linguistic disintegration is evident in Joyce's neologisms and word play while sensual disorientation occurs in the hallucinations of "Circe," which are similar to but more intense than those in *Portrait*. In fact, a drunken Stephen likens his distorted perception to that described in chapter 1 of *Portrait*. Late in "Circe," as Stephen noticeably *"staggers a pace back,"* he admits his disorientation:

> BLOOM: (*propping him*) Retain your own [perpendicularity].
>
> STEPHEN: (*laughs emptily*) My centre of gravity is displaced. I have forgotten the trick. Let us sit down somewhere and discuss. (15.4430–35)

Stephen's sense disorientation from simple intoxication is exacerbated by his missing glasses, lost in circumstances similar to those at Clongowes:

LYNCH: (*watching him*) You would have a better chance of lighting it if you held the match nearer.

STEPHEN: (*brings the match nearer his eye*) Lynx eye. Must get glasses. Broke them yesterday. Sixteen years ago. Distance. The eye sees all flat. (*He draws the match away. It goes out.*) Brain thinks. Near: far. Ineluctable modality of the visible. (15.3624–31)

One is tempted to conclude that the hallucinations of "Circe" are prompted by the general atmosphere of drunkenness, but the hallucinations of Joyce's night world are predominately literary in nature rather than genuine. Only the appearance of Stephen's mother seems to be a genuine hallucination, for most of the others are the product of the sober imagination of Bloom, who has resisted the intoxicating wiles of Circe.

It is precisely this highly literary nature of the hallucinations that distinguishes Joyce's and Barnes's night visions. In the passages quoted above, for instance, Stephen is preoccupied with his disordered senses, but Joyce's aesthetic detachment allows Stephen to parody his earlier, and presumably quite serious, epistemological concerns in "Proteus." So, too, Bloom's fantasies are of a distinctly literary nature; farce, parody, and allusion are the basis for his hallucinations. This is not to say that Bloom's sexual transformations do not represent a genuine attack on the cultural values of contemporary Ireland, but Joyce's technique distances him from such serious questions and lets him skirt the problem of verisimilitude. Bloom's sexual transformations are a sign of Bloom's marginality in his culture.[5] Notwithstanding the importance of that theme in *Ulysses*, Joyce's comic and literary treatment of those fantastic hallucinations provides a dominant counterpoint.

As an Odyssean figure, Bloom quite literally becomes a wandering Jew who, like the Ancient Mariner, remains estranged from the symbolic wedding feast; instead of joining the adulterous Molly, Bloom takes a nocturnal ramble in Dublin's red-light district. With its nighttime setting and Joyce's pervasive use of hallucination, "Circe" provided a model for the world of *Finnegans Wake* which represents a further narrowing or refinement of his night vision. Accordingly, if the structure of a chapter in *Portrait* reflects the overall structure of *Ulysses*, then *Finnegans Wake* may be thought of as an extended nocturnal epiphany. Joyce's last work thus offers the culminating estrangement from the cultural episteme, although its complexity and encyclopedic nature permit only a middle distance examination and selective discussion in this survey of his work.

In *Finnegans Wake* Joyce exhaustively employs every form of disorientation discussed in the introduction of this book. The novel is a dream vision, which, by convention, is an imaginative distortion of daytime sense experience.[6] Essentially, Joyce's journey into the nocturnal world is conceived as an extended subversion and mythopoeic re-creation of the central myth of our culture: the fall from innocence. Joyce describes the fall from grace through a descent into the hypnagogic world of H.C.E. The fall of Humpty Dumpty and the hangover-inspired disorientation that causes the fall of Finnegan become farcical correlatives of the biblical myth in the Christian episteme. The private subversion of the cultural archetype is reinforced by the linguistic playfulness for which the novel is famous. In "The Ondt and the Gracehoper" section, for instance, public myth and private word play are combined within the context of the larger archetype of the fall from grace. Beginning with a well-known parable in which the grasshopper becomes a gracehoper, that is, a fallen creature hoping for grace, Joyce embarks on an etymological and entomological flight. The parable itself all but disappears in the multilingual puns that catalogue insects and insect body parts. While there is hardly a section of *Finnegans Wake* that does not, to some extent, follow this pattern, one chapter is of particular relevance to this study.

The standard, early explications of the novel agree that "Night Lessons" is the central chapter of "the densest part of the *Wake*" (Tindall 171) and perhaps the "most difficult" chapter in the novel (Campbell 62).[7] This chapter, which describes the evening study session of the children of H.C.E. and A.L.P., is a program of lessons covering a wide range of traditional disciplines in the Trivium and Quadrivium of medieval studies: Grammar, Logic, Rhetoric, Arithmetic, Music, Geometry, and Astronomy. The text itself is composed of four parts, which include the lesson, marginal glosses by Shem and Shaun types, and footnotes by Isabel. It is the use of multiple texts that, to a large degree, accounts for the difficulty of the chapter. Like Coleridge's competing texts in "The Ancient Mariner," marginalia and notes in "Night Lessons" compete for the attention of the reader. But in *Finnegans Wake* the reader must listen to four distinct voices whose views on cultural knowledge are at odds with each other. The Shaun voice, initially on the right-hand side in small caps, is solemn, scholarly, and tends to sanctify the lessons. This mental attitude is opposed by the smart-alecky voice of the Shem-type character, who undercuts the seriousness of the exercise. His iconoclastic ally is the sister who, in mock scholarly fashion, supplies humorous footnotes. The difficulty in reading the passage goes beyond the normal linguistic challenge of the novel, for the reader must attempt to balance four differing views on cultural knowledge. As if the reading problem were not already difficult enough, Joyce, near the end of the chapter (293.1), reverses the location of the Shem/Shaun glosses. Further compounding the reader's disorientation, Joyce adds a number of Sternean embellishments to the text. A musical Staff appears in the Shem marginalia (272.130):

B.C. minding missy, please do. But should

Words literally expand and contract (299.36):

greater THaɴ or less ᴛHaN the unitate we

Sigla[8] appear in the footnotes (299.36):

⁴ The Doodles family, ⋔, Δ, ⊣, X, ☐, ⋀, ⊏. Hoodle doodle, fam.?

Geometrical diagrams describe the mother A.L.P.'s womb (293.12):

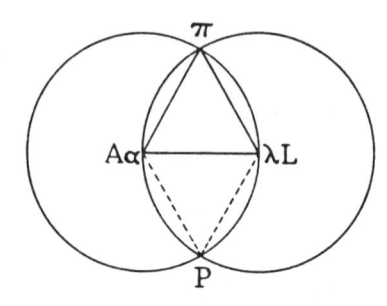

And the chapter closes with Isabel's sketch of a nose being thumbed at the "anticheirst" (308.30–32):

¹ Kish is for anticheirst, and the free of my hand to him!

² And gags for skool and crossbuns and whopes he'll enjoyimsolff over our drawings on the line!

The "Night Lessons" chapter thus provides a radical example of linguistic disorientation in the tradition of "The Ancient Mariner." At the same time, it points to the striking difference between the texture of Joyce's and Barnes's work. While both authors disjoin the cultural episteme through a descent into the night world, Joyce's nocturnal visions reveal great erudition and cultural knowledge even while they subvert this knowledge.

Barnes's Nightwood and the "Evacuation" of Custom

While Barnes, like Joyce, is interested in portraying the phenomenon of sense disorientation and a collapse of social values, her presentation of altered consciousness has more lyric intensity with less use of word play and dramatic farce. *Nightwood* is a sympathetic portrait of those who by their nature, specifically their sensual or sexual nature, depart from the culture's customs and values. Barnes was intimately associated with the sexually liberated crowd of Paris in the twenties and thirties, and her art is centrally concerned with formulating a language and imagery of the night that subverts cultural value. The night world, as a concept, was attractive to Barnes throughout her career. At the age of nineteen, in 1911, Barnes published a poem in *Harper's* entitled "Call of the Night." Anticipating the bestial sympathy expressed in the final scenes of *Nightwood,* the speaker in the poem addresses a canine companion:

> Dark, and the wind-blurred pines,
>   With a glimmer of light between,
> Then I, entombed for an hourless night
>   With a world of things unseen.
>
> Mist, the dust of flowers,
>   Leagues, heavy with promise of snow,
> And a beckoning road 'twixt vale and hill,
>   With the lure that all must know.
>
> A light, my window's gleam,
>   Soft, flaring its squares of red—
> I lose the ache of the wilderness
>   And long for the fire instead.
>
> You too know, old friend?
>   Then, lift up your head and bark.
> It's just the call of the lonesome place,
>   The winds and the housing dark.

Though the mature, poetic prose of *Nightwood* lacks the youthful intensity of these verses, the same passion for the night world pervades her later fiction. Like Joyce's night scenes in *Portrait* and the Nighttown episode of *Ulysses,* Barnes's *Nightwood* has an atmosphere of labyrinthine disorientation that reflects the psychological state of the cultural outcast.

The sensate derangements in *Nightwood*—Felix Volkbein's blindness in one eye (9), Robin Vote's somnambulism which gives her a synesthetic "touch of the blind" (42), Nora Flood's "derangement in her equilibrium" (51), and Dr. Matthew O'Connor's Tiresias-like pronouncements on the "night combed with the great blind searchlight of the heart" (93)—tend to be derangements of the visual sense. The characters in

Nightwood grope blindly on the fringes of Parisian society; their disordered senses reflect their social and cultural disorientation. The world of *Nightwood* is one of dreams and nightmares in which marginal characters become entirely estranged from the culture:

> And what of our own sleep? . . . We are continent a long time, but no sooner has our head touched the pillow, and our eyes left the day, than a host of merrymakers take and get. We wake from our doings in a deep sweat for that they happened in a house without an address, in a street in no town, citizened with people with no names with which to deny them. Their very lack of identity makes them ourselves. (87–88)

The half-dozen characters in *Nightwood* are sleepers, "proprietor[s] of an unknown land," (87) distant from that inhabited by normal citizens whose identity and knowledge is culturally founded. This disjunction is perhaps most clearly seen during Robin Vote's awakening in "La Somnambule," a chapter that draws Barnes's attitudes and techniques into sharp focus. Dr. Matthew O'Connor, an unlicensed gynecologist, has been summoned to the bedside of the young American woman, Robin Vote, who has fallen into a deep, fainting sleep from which she cannot be roused: "On a bed, surrounded by a confusion of potted plants, exotic palms and cut flowers . . . lay the young woman, heavy and dishevelled" (34). Her body exudes a fragrance of decomposition as she slumbers in the embrace of some primal sleep:

> The perfume that her body exhaled was of the quality of that earth-flesh, fungi, which smells of captured dampness and yet is so dry, overcast with the odour of oil of amber, which is an inner malady of the sea, making her seem as if she had invaded a sleep incautious and entire. Her flesh was the texture of plant life, and beneath it one sensed a frame, broad, porous and sleep-worn, as if sleep were a decay fishing her beneath the visible surface. About her head there was an effulgence as of phosphorus glowing about the circumference of a body of

water—as if her life lay through her in ungainly luminous deteriorations—the troubling structure of the born somnambule, who lives in two worlds—meet of child and desperado. (34–35)

The two worlds that Robin inhabits, one of innocence and the other that of a cultural heretic, are not as contradictory as they might seem. Moving among her fellow humans as a somnambulist, Robin, a "beast turning human" (37), is a creature of the night who develops no human ties. Estranged from the fellow men and women of her society, she has no cultural basis for establishing human contact. According to the doctor, she is innocent of social intercourse because "she can't do anything in relation to anyone but herself" (146). Culturally, she exists in a kind of preconscious realm devoid of racial memory, or, as the doctor puts it much later in the novel, "as if the hide of time had been stripped from her, and with it, all transactions with knowledge" (134).

In the scene of Robin's awakening, it is Dr. O'Connor, the physician who has no social sanction for his practice, who delivers Robin from her fainting sleep. During this metamorphosis and birth, the doctor reveals his own marginality as he takes advantage of the unconscious young woman:

> Felix saw that [the doctor's actions were] for the purpose of snatching a few drops from a perfume bottle picked up from the night table; of dusting his darkly bristled chin with a puff, and drawing a line of rouge across his lips, his upper lip compressed on his lower, in order to have it seem that their sudden embellishment was a visitation of nature; still thinking himself unobserved, as if the whole fabric of magic had begun to decompose, as if the mechanics of machination were indeed out of control and were simplifying themselves back to their origin, the doctor's hand reached out and covered a loose hundred franc note lying on the table. (36)

In a curious way, Dr. O'Connor's response to Robin Vote is much like that of Stephen Dedalus to the bird-girl in *Portrait*.

Because of his sexual preference, the doctor is not tempted by Robin's sensuality and provocative posture. Like Stephen's gesture of paring his fingernails, the doctor's rouging and powdering of his face is an autistic and artistic act, a kind of social nonsequitur—the stuff of Leopold Bloom's hallucinations in "Circe" regarding Henry Flower, the "new womanly man."

But the difference between Joyce and Barnes is clear in this scene. Doctor Matthew-Mighty-grain-of-salt-Dante O'Connor is a real "hermaphroditic Irishman" (Weisstein 7) who puts on real make-up and really steals a one-hundred-franc note, whereas Bloom would fantasize such social transgressions. And, replacing thoughts for deeds, Bloom would feel guilty for imagining such illicit actions, while Barnes's character feels not the slightest compunction. The doctor is both practitioner and poet; he is as truly an atomizer of perfume as he is an anatomizer of the night.

The doctor's soliloquies, overheard by Nora in "Watchman, What of the Night?" and in "Go Down Matthew," offer such an "anatomy of night," Barnes's original subtitle for the work (Field 212). The soliloquies illustrate an agile, intellectual association of sensibility that contributes significantly to the linguistic disorientation of the text. The doctor's harangues move from obfuscation to clairvoyance. Substance and sheer fabrication are at war with each other; truth and falsehood compete. Kannenstine aptly summarizes the method of the doctor whose definition and exploration of the night marks his social estrangement from the cultural episteme:

> What actually happens to the narrative as a whole follows from the function of thought sensations and images throughout, from a gradual breakdown of rational and sequential perception. Just as an image emerges from a stop between uncertainties, a dark but universal insight comes out of the static and timeless situation that Nora and the doctor are eventually trapped in. (95)

The text moves from sensation to intellect to abstraction within a single sentence, so that it becomes impossible to isolate various levels of response to experience as we can do so readily in writers like Joyce or Conrad. For the doctor everything occurs in the imaginatively fertile realm of the Prophet of Darkness. The incomprehensible and the comprehensible are yoked to create for the reader a prose poem of fascinating linguistic disorientation.

When Nora Flood enters the doctor's garret at 3 A.M., she enters a setting of estrangement: "So incredible was the disorder that met her eyes. The room was so small that it was just possible to walk sideways up to the bed; it was as if being condemned to the grave the doctor had decided to occupy it with the utmost abandon" (78). Residing in a kind of death chamber, the doctor languishes in a room cluttered with miscellaneously rusted, dirty, and disused medical paraphernalia, with the make-up and soiled underclothes of the transvestite, and with a "swill-pail [that] stood at the head of the bed, brimming with abominations" (79). The doctor himself is nestled in the dirty linen of his bed, nightgowned and heavily rouged, evidently expecting someone besides Nora. In the middle of the night, the doctor has, according to the narrator, "evacuated custom" and has gone back to the female half of his hermaphroditic nature. The doctor explains his transformation in his soliloquy, asserting that "the night is not premeditated" but a series of unstructured sensations that subvert the order superimposed by the intellection of day. The night is a time when personal identity is altered and we each enter a "Town of Darkness," a "secret brotherhood" that cannot be articulated in the light of day. The doctor's utterance, his "nocturnal vision," reflects this incomprehensibility as language itself undergoes an "evacuation of custom":

> His heart is tumbling in his chest, a dark place! Though some go into the night as a spoon breaks easy water, others go ahead foremost against a new connivance; their horns make a dry crying, like the wings of the locust, late come to their shedding. (81)

When reading the Doctor's soliloquies on the night, one is tempted to dismiss them as poetic utterance (or even nonsense) that has no clear, ascertainable meaning. But, as in many recent modern texts, the language of *Nightwood* hovers between denotation and connotation; it simultaneously creates meaning but denies paraphrase. The text, in a sense, competes with and subverts itself. The doctor's soliloquies exist on the fringe of meaning just as the characters of the novel live on the shadowline of society.

A phrase-by-phrase exploration of the possible meanings in the passage above demonstrates the abstract associationism of the doctor's anatomy of night, in which metaphorical meanings compete with each other:

> His heart is tumbling in his chest, a dark place!

The first sentence establishes the connection between the night and human emotions. The line also suggests, through the words "tumbling" and "dark," that night is the realm of passions and emotional chaos, and prepares the reader for the birth imagery that follows.

> Though some go into the night as a spoon breaks easy water,

This introductory clause combines several competing images and metaphors. Breaking water with a spoon suggests the birthing process (with the unorthodox tools of the unlicensed doctor) but also calls to mind breaking wind or urination and, by extension, the pail brimming with abominations at the head of the doctor's bed. This mixture of tropes is repulsive except to those like the doctor for whom the evacuation of custom is compulsive.

> others go head foremost against a new connivance;

The main clause continues the birth metaphor and also suggests the abandonment necessary to plunge into the night world. This phrase "head foremost," unlike the phrases which emphasized the bodily, the sensual, and the excremental, suggests an intellectual plunge into darkness.

> their horns make a dry crying,

The word "horns" suggests the pain of birth and also carries sexual and musical overtones. "Horns" also suggests that the "connivance" may be demonic. "Dry crying" is an oxymoron that, to the hermaphrodite, suggests the sterility of the birth process.

> like the wings of a locust, late come to their shedding.

The simile is poetic embellishment, but it is also in keeping with the transformation of birth and the doctor's practice of changing identity and clothes which is a surrogate birth for him.

The above interpretations are purposefully tentative, for the passage defies a definitive paraphrase. The reader of *Nightwood* and the doctor's soliloquies in particular may choose between competing reading processes: passive enjoyment of the abstractions or an active dissection of the doctor's associative utterance. Barnes exploits this process of breaking down "rational and sequential perception" (Kannenstien 114) throughout much of the doctor's soliloquy, and his language thus reflects his subject.

The competition between opposing forces in the doctor's nocturnal vision is essentially Blakean. He asks Nora "to think of the night the day long, and of the day the night through" (84), for he knows there is no progress without competing, contrary states, without "thinking with the eye that you fear" (83). An understanding of the night world comes only after developing acute nocturnal vision, sensitive to the nuances of shadow and darkness:

> Listen! Do things look in the ten and twelve of noon as they look in the dark? Is the hand, the face, the foot, the same face and hand and foot seen by the sun? For now the hand lies in shadow; its beauties and its deformities are in a smoke—there is a sickle of doubt across the cheek bone thrown by the hat's brim, so there is half a face to be peered back into speculation. A leaf of darkness has fallen under the chin and lies deep upon the arches of the eyes; the eyes themselves have changed their colour. (85)

The doctor advocates disjoining the cultural episteme through an immersion into the destructive element of the night world. Only through a courageous descent into the night can one, conscious or dreaming, become "the proprietor of an unknown land" (87). It is in the night world of dreams that we move beyond the codes of cultural perception into the heretical space of the culturally estranged.

The nocturnal visions that both Barnes and Joyce evoke in their works create an epistemological disorientation that is shared by both character and reader. But differences in mode are clear. Joyce seeks sensate and linguistic disorientation as much for the sake of literary play and parody as for cultural criticism. As a comic writer, Joyce distances himself from the portraits he draws. Barnes, in contrast, maintains a lyric intensity through her confessional tone and Elizabethan diction. This lyricism and tragic seriousness, apparent in Dr. Matthew O'Connor's final deranged utterance, "now *nothing, but wrath and weeping!*" (166), clearly delineates the essential difference between Barnes's and Joyce's nocturnal visions. Barnes's vision ends with tragic desolation while Joyce's *Ulysses* concludes with affirmation and the qualified triumph of human love.

Five
Joseph Conrad and the Shadow-Line of Disorientation

To see! To see!—this is the craving of the sailor, as of the rest of blind humanity. To have his path made clear for him is the aspiration of every human being in our beclouded and tempestuous existence.
—Joseph Conrad, *The Mirror of the Sea*

Though Conrad had no preoccupation with artificially induced states of mind, as did the English romantics and French symbolists, the imagery of his fiction is nearly as extravagant as that of De Quincey, Poe, or Barnes. Conrad was interested in portraying the extraordinary mental states of the cultural outcast. To delineate these outcast characters and their experiences, Conrad drew equally from his personal experience at sea and from the convention of the voyage of sensuous derangement that appeared in the work of his nineteenth-century predecessors. Whether Conrad consciously adopted the conventions of their art is uncertain, but it is clear that he, like his predecessors, was preoccupied with exceptional mental states and felt a peculiar kinship with these authors regarding their literary careers. In a 1905 letter to Edmund Gosse, Conrad writes of being troubled by periods of creative inertia and sterility: "I need not tell you that this moral support of belief is the greatest help a writer can receive in those difficult moments which Baudelaire has defined happily as *'les stérilités des écrivains nerveux.'* [De] Quincey too, I believe, has known that anguished suspension of all power of thought" (Jean-Aubry 2:14). The mental state of which Conrad speaks not only reflects his psychological condition as an artist, it is an apt de-

---

This chapter, in slightly different form, first appeared in *Conradiana* as "The Sensationist Epistemology in Conrad's Early Fiction" (16) 1984: 3–18, and as "Conrad's Voyages of Disorientation: Crossing the Shadow-Line" (17) 1985: 83–92.

scription of the extraordinary physical sensations recorded on his voyages of disorientation. During these voyages, character and reader journey across both physical and psychological shadow-lines, away from the culturally familiar and into a heretical landscape.

While the bulk of Conrad's fiction depicts some kind of disorienting journey from cultural knowledge, no single work treats the theme of cultural disintegration more centrally or explicitly than *The Secret Agent*. Written when Conrad's personal life was at a low point, this darkly ironic tale depicts the disintegration of social value and order. The novel is peopled by characters who, like those of Joyce or Barnes, operate on the fringe of society; but unlike the revellers in the "Circe" chapter of *Ulysses* or the sensualists in *Nightwood,* Conrad's London anarchists seek the disintegration of moral order as an end in itself. Although many of the so-called anarchists are portrayed as pathetically ineffectual—as patrons of destruction rather than as destructive men—the Professor in *Secret Agent,* who seeks "the disintegration of the old morality, . . . a clean sweep and a clear start for a new conception of life" (Conrad 1926, 13:73), is depicted as dangerous. The great danger of the Professor is that he pursues his heretical vision with "frenzied puritanism of ambition. He nursed it as something secularly holy" (13:81). The practical ambition of the Professor to create the perfect detonator is ironically realized when the half-witted Stevie trips and is instantaneously dismembered and fragmented, becoming "a heap of rags, scorched and bloodstained, half concealing what might have been an accumulation of raw material for a cannibal feast" (13:86). Conrad's use of cannibalism, like that in *The Narrative of Arthur Gordon Pym,* expresses the disintegration of cultural value. Like Poe, Conrad disjoins the cultural episteme through an analogous disintegration of human flesh and moral order.

While *The Secret Agent* provides the most obvious thematic treatment of a disintegrated cultural or moral order, the novel is eccentric within the body of Conrad's fiction which more often disjoins the cultural episteme through the use of allegory or symbolism. Typically, Conrad employs the convention of the disorienting journey, which leads character, narrator, and reader to a point of sensual, cognitive, or psychological derangement. Marlow's remark at the beginning of *Heart of Darkness* that his journey to meet Kurtz "was the farthest point of navigation and the culminating point of [his] experience" (16:51) illustrates the widely accepted view that Conrad's geographical journeys are also psychological journeys. Because Conrad often stated that the duty of the artist is to descend within himself (*Prefaces* 49–50), it is perhaps natural for the reader to concentrate attention on defining the nature of Conrad's spiritual or psychological voyages of discovery. But to dwell on the psychological world and ignore the character's or narrator's response to the sensate world is to risk a fundamental misunderstanding of how Conrad most commonly structures his symbolic voyages,[1] and how he continues the conventions of the heretical symbolist voyage of disorientation.

In much of Conrad's work—like that of Coleridge, De Quincey, and Rimbaud—the journeyer undergoes an extraordinary sense experience which immediately precedes and sometimes causes an altered awareness of self and humankind in relation to the universe. Conrad's disorienting voyages are journeys away from the culturally familiar; his tales are about physical and psychic exile. Whether the moment of sensate derangement he describes involves synesthesia, anesthesia, visual clouding, or tempestuous kinesthetic disorder, this moment of "uncommon or personal sensation" (17:3) represents the crossing of a "shadow-line" that severs the voyager from the cultural episteme.

Early in his career, Conrad seemed pained by the realization that his tales were generated not by ideas but by sensations. He complained in an 1896 letter to Edward Garnett of having no "starting point" as he imagined other writers did: "They know something to begin with—while I don't. I have had some impressions, some sensations—in my time:—impressions and sensations of common things" (Garnett 38). Conrad's admission suggests not only that he was interested in writing about his experiences, but more importantly that, as an artist, Conrad depended less on cultural knowledge than on direct sensual experience. In later years, when his success as a man of letters was confirmed, Conrad spoke with more assurance about the sources of his writing: "My work shall not be an utter failure because it has the solid basis of a definite intention. . . . In its essence it is action . . . nothing but action—action observed, felt and interpreted with an absolute truth to my sensations (which are the basis of art in literature)" (Blackwood 155–56).

When Conrad asserts the primacy of sensation in his literary-epistemological process, he admits the heresy of the empiricist, who immerses himself in the density of a physical world and is implicitly free of any divine order. Like a sensationalist or a positivist, Conrad thought of himself as an artist who sought to define—in concrete and not impressionistic terms[2]—the fundamental nature of reality. Although Conrad's temperament was far from scientific and his mind far from systematic and disciplined in the manner of a positivist thinker, Conrad could be quite enthusiastic about scientific concepts of sensation. In a letter dated 29 September 1898, Conrad tells Edward Garnett of a scientific discussion he enjoyed in Scotland. The discussion revolved around "*the* secret of the universe" which is "composed of the same matter, matter, *all matter* being only that thing of inconceivable tenuity through which the various vibrations of waves (electricity, heat, sound, light, etc.) are propagated, thus giving birth to our sensations—then emotions—then thoughts. Is that so?" (Garnett 136). Conrad's tag question surely reveals his uneasiness in dealing with such problematical "matters of fact," yet his interest in them and his admission that the scientist, thinker, and artist seek the same truths using different methods (*Prefaces* 49–50) are testimony of his keen, if naive, interest in the positivist tenets of sensationalist thinking, which was flourishing in Europe at the time.

There is no reason to suspect that Conrad ever read any of the sensationalist thinkers. Though it is remotely possible that Conrad could have been introduced to the latest theories of physiological perception by his medical-student tutor, Pulman, this is highly improbable, for the young Conrad neither enjoyed nor rigorously pursued his studies which were often interrupted by illness and ultimately discontinued in favor of travel (Karl 88ff.). It is thus unlikely that Conrad had either formal or informal exposure to philosophical sensationalism, but rather developed an artistic sensibility and aesthetic epistemology that mirrored the philosophic concerns of his age. Conrad's statement of artistic intent in the Preface to *The Nigger of the "Narcissus,"* however, expresses many of the major concerns of the sensationalist thinkers of the time, particularly those of Ernst Mach. Mach's *Analysis of The Sensations* (1896), a translation of *Beiträge zur Analyse der Empfindungen* (1885), explores the relation between the physical and psychical worlds. This basic sensationalist concern is at the heart of Conrad's artistic intent: "My task which I am trying to achieve is, by the power of the written word to make you hear, to make you feel—it is, before all, to make you *see*" (*Prefaces* 52). Conrad's emphasis on the word *see* implies not only visual sensation but perception and knowledge as well. The coalescence of image and knowledge—a collapsing of the distinction between external stimuli and internal response—emphasizes the primacy of sensation as a way of knowing. Conrad's position is thus closely aligned with that of the sensationalists which is essentially heretical in nature, depending neither on Logos nor revelation but rather on direct sensate experience as the primary way of knowing.

Conrad's sensationalist episteme is evident in the well-known opening lines of the preface to *The Nigger of the "Narcissus"* which states that art should be "a single-minded attempt to render the highest kind of justice to the visible universe." Conrad proceeds, suggesting that the artist, in describing the visible universe, attempts "to find in its form, in its colours, in its light, in its shadows, in the aspects of matter, and in the facts of life what of each is fundamental, what is enduring and essential—their one illuminating and convincing quality—the very truth of their existence" (*Prefaces* 49). Those critics who label Conrad an impressionist frequently cite this passage as evidence of a kind of painterly aesthetic.[3] But it is surprisingly like Mach's definition of sensation as the individual's transmuting of the physical elements of the phenomenal world into thought and knowledge of that world.[4] Mach explains the nature of phenomenal reality by theorizing that objects or bodies, though interpreted by the perceiving mind as whole "things" are actually complexes of individual sensations. As a phenomenologist, Mach seeks "to render the highest kind of justice to the visible universe," and, as an artist, Conrad stresses sensation as a way of knowing because "all art . . . appeals primarily to the senses" (*Prefaces* 51). When the artist takes a less direct approach, the understanding we bring away from art is less "enduring and essential."

To render justice to the visible universe Conrad thus develops a sensationalist literary epistemology, dependent less on cultural givens than direct sensate experience. Like Mach, who posits three levels of perceptual response involving "sensation, intuition, phantasy" (Mach 1976, 105–19), Conrad explores the epistemological process as "action observed, felt, and interpreted" in a narrative that delineates first "sensations—then emotions—then thoughts." The connection between this sensationalist epistemology and the literary imagination is clearly articulated by Conrad in an 1895 letter to Edward Noble:

> You must treat events only as illustrative of human sensation,—as the outward sign of inward feelings,—of live feelings,—which alone are truly pathetic and interesting. . . . To accomplish it you must cultivate your poetic faculty,—you must give yourself up to emotions (no easy task). You must squeeze out of yourself every sensation, every thought, every image—mercilessly, without reserve and without remorse. (Jean-Aubry 1:183)

In the remainder of the letter Conrad reiterates the order of the three responses to experience: sensation, knowledge, and image. This careful emphasis clearly suggests the importance Conrad attached to this modified Aristotelian triad as the foundation of his theory of the literary imagination. More importantly, this order of response indicates his epistemological process and, as we will see, provided a basic structure for his fiction: Extraordinary sensations lead to knowledge or altered awareness which leads to a visionary moment.

Sensation, Knowledge, Image

The term *sensation* is pervasive in Conrad's fiction. As the most immediate, fundamental response to the experiential world, sensation implies, quite simply, the excitation of the senses. But in Conrad's work sensation can also describe the apprehension of space and time or the "feelings" of pain or exhilaration or even joy, as it does in sensationalist theory (Mach 1897, 7–8). Though the word is applied broadly, it is used consistently to denote a prerational, even preconscious, response to experience. Because of the primacy of sensation in his epistemology, Conrad often denies his characters any rational reflection on events, which are presented to the reader as uninterpreted phenomena. "An Outpost of Progress" offers a good example of this technique. A particularly interesting passage occurs in the text just after Kayerts and Carlier resolve their disagreement:

> All at once he heard the other push his chair back; and he leaped to his feet with extreme facility. He listened and got confused. Must run again! Right or Left? He heard footsteps. He darted to the left, grasping his revolver, and at the very same instant, as it seemed to him, they came into violent collision. Both shouted with surprise. A loud explosion took place between them; a roar of red fire, thick smoke; and Kayerts, deafened and blinded, rushed back thinking: 'I am hit—it's all over.' He expected the other to come round—to gloat over his agony. He caught hold of an upright of the roof—'All over!' Then he heard a crashing fall on the other side of the house, as if somebody had tumbled headlong over a chair—then silence. Nothing more happened. He did not die. (8:112–13)

In using Kayerts as a central consciousness, Conrad stresses the difference between sensation and thought and also shows that in an uninitiated or stupid individual the gap between sensation and thought is dangerously large. Edward Said makes the more sweeping generalization that in Conrad's short fiction "action of any sort is either performed or witnessed without accompanying reflection or interpretation, as if the overriding and immediate sensation of action done to, by, or in front of one crowds out the informing work of reason" (87). Working with the same passage from "Outpost" to define Conrad's impressionism, Ian Watt similarly concludes that "one of the devices that [Conrad] hit on was to present a sense impression and withhold naming it or examining its meaning until later; as readers we witness every step by which the gap between individual perception and its cause is belatedly closed within the consciousness of the protagonist" (175). Watt's terminology, however, is somewhat misleading. Since perception often implies conscious apprehension and rational interpretation, the term *sensation* or *percept* is more useful here as it implies only that one is sensible of phenomena. As Watt himself later says, "Conrad's main objective is to put us into intense sensory contact with the events; and this objective means that the physical impression must precede the understanding of cause" (178). This certainly is Conrad's point. The gap between sensation and perception is an indicator of the nature and quality of a character's epistemological process, a process in which the reader is simultaneously engaged.

Kayerts and Carlier are "incapable individuals" either because the gap between sensation and perception is too large or, worse, because no real perception occurs. In fact, the pair are so unreceptive to experience that at times sensations themselves, particularly unfamiliar ones, make little impact. Conrad describes them as two "blind men in a large room, aware only of what came in contact with them (and of that only imperfectly)" (8:92). The downfall of Kayerts and Carlier stems from their failure to apprehend the warnings of impending disaster transmitted by their senses. After the threatening strangers intrude upon their station, Kayerts and Carlier ignore all evidence of their perilous situation:

There was some talk about keeping a watch in turn, but in the evening everything seemed so quiet and peaceful that they retired as usual. All night they were disturbed by a lot of drumming in the villages. A deep, rapid roll near by would be followed by another far off—then all ceased. Soon short appeals would rattle out here and there, then all mingle together, increase, become vigorous and sustained, would spread out over the forest, roll though the night, unbroken and ceaseless, near and far, as if the whole land had been one immense drum booming out steadily an appeal to heaven. And through the deep and tremulous noise sudden yells that resembled snatches of songs from a madhouse darted shrill and high in discordant jets of sound which seemed to rush far above the earth and drive all peace from under the stars.
Carlier and Kayerts slept badly. (8:98–99)

Conrad portrays their numbness to the experiential world by presenting uninterpreted sense data to the reader. The lack of authorial comment, used so frequently in this ironic tale, here emphasizes the distance between the characters' and the reader's understanding. Having expressed satisfaction with what seems to be true and having consciously elected not to keep watch, the uninquisitive, semiconscious pair experience a night of disturbed sleep which is the counterpart of their somnambulant workdays.

Lord Jim is another character who sees imperfectly. When assassins lurk in his *campong,* Jim remains unaware of their presence and depends on Jewel to see for him. As Jim walks to the storeroom to face the assassins whom he does not believe exist, the "dense blackness" of the night is not threatening but rather a "friendly beauty" (21:298). Nor is Jim threatened when "something dark, imperfectly seen, flitted rapidly out of sight." Jim is still unconvinced of the presence of danger, even when he enters the storehouse (lit by Jewel):

'He pushed violently; the door swung with a creak and a clatter, disclosing to his intense astonishment the low dungeon-like interior illuminated by a lurid, wavering glare. A turmoil of smoke eddied down upon an empty wooden crate in the middle of the floor, a litter of rags tried to soar, but only stirred feebly in the draught.' (21:300)

Jim's failure to respond to the visual sensation of the stirring rag heap nearly causes his death: " 'He had perceived in the very act of turning away that he was exchanging glances with a pair of eyes in the heap of mats. . . . Next moment the whole mound stirred, and with a low grunt a man emerged swiftly, and bounded towards Jim' " (21:301). Throughout the novel, Jim's physical sensibilities, and consequently his ability to perceive, are permanently deranged by his jump from the *Patna*. Jim's disorientation of the senses leads to his retreat from the world and his inability to see that world realistically. He is doomed to reenact the fall until near the end of his life when he finally accepts the consequences of his action: " 'Then Jim understood. He had retreated from one world, for a small matter of an impulsive jump, and now the other, the work of his own hands [his life at *Patusan*], had fallen in ruins upon his head' " (21:408).

Jim's and Kayert's shortcomings as sentient beings contrast with the potential of a pair like Nostromo and Decoud. While Kayerts and Carlier operate blindly in the full light of day and Jim fails to "see" by torchlight, Nostromo and Decoud initially seem capable of heroic action because of their heightened states of physiological perception. In the perfect darkness of the Placid Gulf, they execute their escape from Sulaco "like a pair of blind men aware of each other and their surroundings by some indefinable sixth sense" (9:296). Like Kayerts and Carlier, they are blind men doomed to fail, yet they are superior in kind to these two characters because of their physiological sensitivity to each other and their surroundings which makes them more capable of handling their immediate experience. The distinction between sensation and thought is explicit in Conrad's description of Decoud's response to the lighter's brush with the steamer: "For the space of two or three gasping breaths that new rope held against the sudden strain. It was this that gave Decoud the sensation of the snatching pull, dragging the lighter away to destruction. The cause of it, of course, was inexplicable to him. The whole thing was so sudden that he had no time to think. But all his sensations were perfectly clear" (9:292). Decoud shows an immediate and sure apprehension of sensate experience, and there is only a brief gap between sensation and understanding. There is a similarly short delay in decoding the data of the senses in *Heart of Darkness* (Ian Watt 175). Marlow sees his "poleman give up the business suddenly, and stretch himself flat on the deck, without even taking the trouble to haul his pole in" (16:109), and then sees "sticks, little sticks . . . flying about." After a delay of several seconds, Marlow divests himself of his cultural perception and realizes, in a quasi-comical way, that the sticks are arrows and that his steamer is under attack.

The second stage of Conrad's theory of the literary imagination, the second level of response to experience, is the translation of sensation into rational perception. Although this process may at first seem self-evident, many of Conrad's characters are defined by whether or not they are capable of creative thought as a response to sensation. For Conrad, a character's success in the experiential world is based on the character's perceptual faculties and thought processes. On this point, Conrad is closely allied with the sensationalist position. In sensationalist thought sensations are experienced on a preconscious level: "By sensations are exited, in animals, the movements of adaptation demanded by their conditions of life" (Mach 1897, 82). Sensation impinges on the animal or human in a fundamental and prerational way. Mach further asserts that in intelligent species— presumably including man—"the parts of these complexes necessary to produce the excitation constantly diminish, and the sensations are more and more supplemented and replaced by the intellect, as may be daily observed in children and adolescent animals" (83–84). Sensationalist thinkers thus posit two avenues of knowledge in humans: the direct sensuous one and an intellectual one that is further removed from sensate experience. Mach warns that one level of knowing does not absolutely replace the other and that the two must work in tandem: "Representation by images and ideas, therefore, has to supply the place of sensations, where the latter are imperfect, and to carry to their issue processes initially determined by sensations alone. But in normal life, representation cannot *supplant* sensation, where this is at all present, except with the greatest danger to the organism" (Mach 1897, 84).

In Conrad's fiction, when a character's knowledge is divorced from sensate experience by either habit or sustained withdrawal into the intellect, the individual often fails to prosper and may eventually even die. Conversely, the characters who remain in touch with their senses have a better knowledge of their immediate circumstances and thus a better chance of survival.

Kayerts and Carlier are an obvious example of characters who fail to prosper due to the disjunction between sensation and thought. Because Kayerts and Carlier are all but insensible for the better part of the story, they are also untroubled by any real mental activity, any real thought. As creatures of civilization, their "every great and every insignificant thought" belongs not to them "but to the crowd" (8:89). It is only through Kayerts's unavoidable confrontation with the undeniable fact of "a pair of white naked feet in red slippers" (8:113) that he finally realizes, to his horror, that "he had shot an unarmed man" (8:114). Conversely, Martin Decoud is an example of a man totally absorbed in audaciously skeptical thought. He is capable of such immersion in thought because he is particularly susceptible to empirical sensations. But the sensuous overstimulation of the Placid Gulf, followed by the island solitude of the Great Isabel, proves dangerous:

> The enormous stillness, without light or sound, seemed to affect Decoud's senses like a powerful drug. He didn't even know at times whether he were asleep or awake. Like a man lost in slumber, he heard nothing, he saw nothing. Even his hand held before his face did not exist for his eyes. The change from the agitation, the passions and the dangers, from the sights and sounds of the

shore, was so complete that it would have resembled death had it not been for the survival of his thoughts. In this foretaste of eternal peace they floated vivid and light, like unearthly clear dreams of earthly things that may haunt the souls freed by death from the misty atmosphere of regrets and hopes. (9:262)

Here, the absence of sensuous stimuli is itself experienced as a kind of hyperesthetic synesthesia. Hearing nothing and seeing nothing, Decoud becomes sensuously disoriented. The stillness assumes an "enormous" size, and the unseen hand held in front of his face ceases to exist for the skeptical Decoud. In the absence of all sensation, only his thoughts remain and, consequently, he is in great danger.

This dichotomy between "perceptive" and "imperceptive" characters is readily apparent in *Typhoon,* though in this tale Conrad treats the issue comically. On the one hand, Captain MacWhirr is wonderfully out of touch with the world of the senses. He is so mistrustful of and lacking in empirical knowledge that he never has an imaginative thought. Conrad describes him as a man who has "just enough imagination to carry him through each successive day, and no more" (20:4). As skipper of the *Nana-Shan,* MacWhirr is first introduced examining a meteorological instrument: "He stood confronted by the fall of a barometer he had no reason to distrust. The fall—taking into account the excellence of the instrument, the time of the year, and the ship's position on the terrestrial globe—was of a nature ominously prophetic" (20:6). His conclusion that "there must be some uncommonly dirty weather knocking about" and the verbal poverty he exhibits by repeating the phrase reveal a corresponding mental impoverishment. And yet ironically MacWhirr's limitations and inadequacies are the very qualities that save the ship. Far from constituting a shift in Conrad's epistemology, which stresses the need for sharpened senses and creative thought in the face of danger, the triumph of MacWhirr's ineptitude is simply an artistic variation in tone and mode. The positive results of MacWhirr's bookishness are both ironic and comic.

Jukes, in the same story, provides yet another comic inversion. Though Jukes's empirical observations of the weather are decidedly more acute than MacWhirr's, he is portrayed as neither unusually intelligent nor imaginative. Before the passage where Jukes makes an entry into the ship's log, Conrad describes the evening in painterly images: "The coppery twilight retired slowly, and the darkness brought out overhead a swarm of unsteady, big stars, that, as if blown upon, flickered exceedingly and seemed to hang very near the earth" (20:26). The dense sensuous imagery is an appropriate prelude to the scene that follows:

> He copied neatly out of the rough-book the number of miles, the course of the ship, and in the column for 'wind' scrawled the word 'calm' from top to bottom of the eight hours since noon. He was exasperated by the continuous, monotonous rolling of the ship. The heavy inkstand would slide away in a manner that suggested perverse intelligence in dodging the pen. Having written in the large space under the head of 'Remarks' 'Heat very oppressive,' he stuck the end of the penholder in his teeth, pipe fashion, and mopped his face carefully.
> 'Ship rolling heavily in a high cross swell,' he began again, and commented to himself, 'Heavily is no word for it.' Then he wrote; 'Sunset threatening, with a low bank of clouds to N. and E. Sky clear overhead.'
> Sprawling over the table with arrested pen, he glanced out of the door, and in that frame of his vision he saw all the stars flying upwards between the teakwood jambs on a black sky. The whole lot took flight together and disappeared, leaving only a blackness flecked with white flashes, for the sea was as black as the sky and speckled with foam afar. The stars that had flown to the roll came back on the return swing of the ship, rushing downwards in their glittering multitude, not of fiery points, but enlarged to tiny discs brilliant with a clear wet sheen.
> Jukes watched the flying big stars for a moment, and then wrote: '8 P.M. Swelling increasing. Ship la-

bouring and taking water on her decks. Battened down the coolies for the night. Barometer still falling.' (20:26–27)

Like MacWhirr, Jukes must be concerned with factual data, but when he records these observations, he is quick to add details based on personal sense experience. His word choices reveal an evaluation of the situation: "calm" to describe the wind, "heat very oppressive" to indicate temperature and atmospheric conditions, and "ship rolling heavily" beneath a "threatening sunset." These comments reveal an active, interpreting mind that is not only sensible of the phenomenal world but also depends on direct sensations to imaginatively recreate reality. Immediately after Jukes's notation of these observations, the omniscient narrator describes the stars which appear to fly upwards and downwards with the rolling of the ship. The sense data that the reader receives is unadorned and uninterpreted, for Conrad presents a vivid but objective description of the stars rushing from bottom to top and top to bottom of the door which frames the outside world, much like De Quincey's perceptual frames. Immediately, Jukes translates this sense experience into a rational evaluation of the storm's progress: "Swelling increasing." To make sure that the reader is aware of Jukes's epistemological process, Conrad ends the scene with a dramatic rendering of Jukes's mental activity as he struggles to read the signs of the coming storm and to reconcile himself to its reality: "'Barometer still falling.' He paused, and thought to himself, 'Perhaps nothing whatever'll come of it.' And then he closed resolutely his entries: 'Every appearance of a typhoon coming on'" (20:27).

The level of knowledge that is most difficult to achieve is, according to Conrad's epistemology, like sensation, a nonrational experience. But unlike sensation, which is prerational, this ultimate knowledge which Marlow calls the "culminating point of [his] experience" is a transrational, visionary image. It exists apart from sensuous apprehension, rational understanding, or even verbal articulation and typically involves a character's defining his self in relation to the universe. This knowledge is made manifest by the author in an "image" that he retrieves from deep within himself. As Conrad advises Edward Noble, "you must search the darkest corners of your heart, the most remote recesses of your brain,—you must search them for the image" (Jean-Aubry 1:183). When Conrad speaks of the image, it is likely that he means something similar to but by no means identical to the common notion of image. Rather, he is describing the image which inheres in the visionary moment, something like Coleridge's symbolic involution, De Quincey's involute, Baudelaire's *correspondances*, or Joyce's epiphany. As Conrad and his characters illustrate, this type of image, though literally expressed through sensation and thought, transcends both and manifests itself in a single symbolic expression such as an imaginatively conceived situation, a secular icon expressing a moral ideal, an ambience or allegorical setting, or another similar visionary summation of experience.

Marlow, in *Lord Jim,* provides a convenient definition of the Conradian moment of vision and its relation to the senses:

> 'It's extraordinary how we go through life with eyes half shut, with dull ears, with dormant thoughts. Perhaps it's just as well; and it may be that it is this very dulness that makes life to the incalculable majority so supportable and so welcome. Nevertheless, there can be but few of us who had never known one of these rare moments of awakening when we see, hear, understand ever so much—everything—in a flash—before we fall back again into our agreeable somnolence.' (21:1423)

It is the recollection of the moment of vision, the poignant memory of this rare moment, that forms the basis of the Conradian image. In many ways, Marlow's last view of Lord Jim provides the clearest and most interesting example of this visionary image, interesting because it suggests an identification between Conrad the novelist and Marlow the yarn spinner. Like Conrad, who starts a tale with "definite images," Marlow is obsessed by his final iconic vision of Jim:

> 'For me that white figure in the stillness of coast and sea seemed to stand at the heart of a vast enigma. The twi-

light was ebbing fast from the sky above his head, the strip of sand had sunk already under his feet, he himself appeared no bigger than a child—then only a speck, a tiny white speck, that seemed to catch all the light left in a darkened world. . . . And suddenly, I lost him. . . . ' (21:336).

In this image, which is repeated several times in the novel (21:175, 393), Conrad is able to sum up the temperament of the romantic *Tuan* Jim, the ambience of Patusan, and the human condition as expressed by the outcast in an alien land. Marlow's image of Jim is thus a symbolic expression of the entire novel.

Though other images in Conrad's work are not quite as central to their respective tales or novels, these visionary moments are usually existential in nature and are frequently the culminating point in the character's life. Often they are directly associated with a character's mortality and either are brought on by thoughts of death or bring on death itself when the image proves too terrifying, as in the case of the skeptical Decoud and the unimaginative Kayerts. On the Great Isabel, Decoud finds these visionary images fatal: "Not a living being, not a speck of a distant sail, appeared within the range of his vision; and, as if to escape from this solitude, he absorbed himself in his melancholy. . . . His sadness was the sadness of a sceptical mind. He beheld the universe as a succession of incomprehensible images" (9:498). In a man who "recognized no other virtue than intelligence," the incomprehensibility of these images, evoked by solitude and magnified by loss of sleep, leads to suicide. Kayerts has a similar experience in "Outpost." Like Decoud, he is a character who has lived a "misdirected life" by recognizing no virtue other than familiarity. As Decoud has sublimated his passion and humanity in favor of skeptical intellection, so Kayerts has ignored the imaginative intellect for the security of the habitual. With the murder of Carlier, however, this changes:

Night came, and Kayerts sat unmoving on his chair. He sat quiet as if he had taken a dose of opium. The vio-

> lence of the emotions he had passed through produced a feeling of exhausted serenity. He had plumbed in one short afternoon the depths of horror and despair, and now found repose in the conviction that life had no more secrets for him: neither had death! He sat by the corpse thinking; . . . thinking very new thoughts. . . . His old thought, convictions, likes and dislikes, things he respected and things he abhorred, appeared in their true light at last! . . . He, Kayerts, was a thinking creature. He had been all his life, till that moment, a believer in a lot of nonsense like the rest of mankind—who are fools; but now he thought! He Knew! He was at peace; he was familiar with the highest wisdom! (8:114–15)

Though obviously ironic, this passage nonetheless contains a darkly comic element of truth. The extraordinary sense experiences that accompany the act of murdering Carlier rouse Kayerts from his waking sleep. He is for the first time engaged in genuine thought. But this intellectual breakthrough, clichéd though it is, leads to a terrifying vision: "Then he tried to imagine himself dead, and Carlier sitting in his chair watching him; and his attempt met with such unexpected success, that in a very few moments he became not at all sure who was dead and who was alive" (8:115). Were "Outpost" written after *Nostromo,* Kayerts would be an ironic parody of Decoud as he grapples with an incomprehensible image. Kayerts's image of his own death is impossible for him to bear.

There are, of course, Conradian characters who benefit from or even triumph in their experience with such images. Singleton in *The Nigger of the "Narcissus,"* for example, has a visionary experience which reconciles him to his mortality. Because of his sensibility and experience, the image is a profitable summation of his life as a seaman:

> He looked upon the immortal sea with the awakened and groping perception of its heartless might; he saw it unchanged, black and foaming under the eternal scrutiny of the stars; he heard its impatient voice calling for him out of a pitiless vastness full of unrest, of turmoil,

and of terror. He looked afar upon it, and he saw an immensity tormented and blind, moaning and furious, that claimed all the days of his tenacious life, and, when life was over, would claim the worn-out body of its slave.... (23:99)

His vision is triumphant because it ends in what Conrad calls "completed wisdom," a transcendent understanding of human mortality in a vast and indifferent universe. In *Heart of Darkness,* too, the image or vision of the central character is the culmination of human experience. In that tale, Kurtz has a paradoxically triumphant vision of human failure. During this undefined epiphany, Marlow sees an expression of pride, power, and terror on Kurtz's face and wonders:

"Did he live his life again in every detail of desire, temptation, and surrender during the supreme moment of complete knowledge? He cried in a whisper at some image, at some vision—he cried out twice, a cry that was no more than a breath—
" 'The horror! The horror!' " (16:149)

Despite Kurtz's shortcomings, Marlow believes that Kurtz achieves a "victory" because the European, having defamiliarized his vision of the world and himself, sees beyond his blind idealism and acquires "complete knowledge."

Conrad's sensationalist epistemology is thus both a key to the mental lives of his characters and a model for structuring dramatic scenes and narrative events. His characters typically illustrate a three-stage epistemological process, beginning with a disorienting voyage of unusual sensual experiences which lead to a new, rational understanding of the world or human experience. This new knowledge, in turn, leads to a transrational image or vision through which the character apprehends a higher truth about reality and achieves a still deeper understanding of the human condition.

These three stages of the epistemological process—sensation, thought, and image—are often compressed into a relatively short fictional space and leave little doubt that Conrad meant to juxtapose these responses to the phenomenal world. One illustrative passage comes from one of Conrad's late works, near the beginning of Section 3 of *The Shadow-Line* when the narrator, a captain, boards his first command:

> The mahogany table under the skylight shone in the twilight like a dark pool of water. The sideboard, surmounted by a wide looking-glass in an ormolu frame, had a marble top. . . . The saloon itself was panelled in two kinds of wood in the excellent, simple taste prevailing when the ship was built.
> I sat down in the arm-chair. . . .
> A succession of men had sat in that chair. I became aware of that thought suddenly, vividly, as though each had left a little of himself between the four walls of these ornate bulkheads; as if a sort of composite soul, the soul of command, had whispered suddenly. . .
> 'You too!' it seemed to say, 'you too, shall taste of that peace and that unrest in a searching intimacy with your own self—obscure as we were and as supreme in the face of all the winds and all the seas, in an immensity that receives no impress, preserves no memories, and keeps no reckoning of lives.' (17:52–53)

The first paragraph of the passage describes the new captain's sensations, primarily visual, as he enters the saloon for the first time; the third short paragraph relates his thoughts about taking over the command; and the fourth paragraph translates those thoughts into a more cosmic image of the voyage of the soul. Here, in the space of around two hundred words, Conrad expresses in the order they occur all three modes of perception. Elsewhere, Conrad deals more extensively with these three levels of response, structuring his tales and novels around a critical, sensually disorienting event that severs the journeyer from what is culturally known. Knowing what is unknown to others in his culture, the disoriented voyager becomes a cultural heretic.

The Disorienting Voyage

Perhaps the most obvious example of the disorienting voyage is in *The Shadow-Line*. In the dead calm of the Gulf of Siam, the narrator experiences a near total loss of sensation that disorients him: "My command might have been a planet flying vertiginously on its appointed path in a space of infinite silence. I clung to the rail as if my sense of balance were leaving me for good" (17:74). The crew and captain are caught in a "life-in-death" state like the one known to Coleridge's Ancient Mariner; the normal aural, kinesthetic, and visual senses are negated in the absence of stimulation. The narrator remarks that "the brooding stillness of the world seemed sensitive to the slightest sound like a whispering gallery" (17:101). While Conrad may not have been thinking specifically of De Quincey's *Confessions* in this passage, he is fascinated with sensate extremes similar to those that preoccupied the opium-eater. During the calm, starless nights in the Gulf of Siam, the captain, his visual sense impaired, finds himself in an atmosphere of unreality: "Such must have been the darkness before creation. . . . I knew I was invisible to the man at the helm. Neither could I see anything. . . . Every form was gone, too, spar, sail, fittings, rails; everything was blotted out in the dreadful smoothness of that absolute night" (17:113). This catalogue of absences is followed by a description of disconnected visual and kinesthetic experiences which are normally combined aboard ship:

> The ship had no steerage way. She lay with her head to the westward, the everlasting Koh-ring visible over the stern, with a few small islets, black spots in the great blaze, swimming before my troubled eyes. And but for those bits of land there was no speck on the sky, no speck on the water, no shape of vapour, no wisp of smoke, no sail, no boat, no stir of humanity, no sign of life, nothing! (17:95–96)

In the absence of the motion of sailing, the islands themselves, the only visual stimulus, swim before the troubled eyes of the narrator. Conventional perception is stripped away, as the captain confronts the unfamiliar.

The disorientation of the senses that Conrad describes in *The Shadow-Line* is analogous to the experiences of Nostromo and Decoud in the Placid Gulf. For them, too, their very existence is called into question by the anesthetic quietness, darkness, and windlessness of the Sulaco harbor and gulf: "When [Nostromo's] voice ceased, the enormous stillness, without light or sound, seemed to affect Decoud's senses like a powerful drug. He didn't even know at times whether he were asleep or awake. Like a man lost in slumber, he heard nothing, he saw nothing. Even his hand held before his face did not exist for his eyes" (9:262). As if he were entering an opium dream, Decoud crosses a shadow-line to a state of exile on the Great Isabel and faces a crisis in his philosophic skepticism; the universe becomes a "succession of incomprehensible images." For Nostromo, too, the Placid Gulf serves as a shadow-line. Once the silver has been hidden, once he has taken his night journey and is archetypically reborn (Rosenfield 43ff.), he has a new perception of himself, of his career, and of those who have used him. He realizes his corruption.

Scenes involving fog in Conrad's works may also induce a state of anesthesia in a character which is followed by new awareness or understanding. The most poignant example of this is Marlow's encounter with fog immediately below Kurtz's station:[5]

> 'Not the faintest sound of any kind could be heard. You looked on amazed and began to suspect yourself of being deaf—then the night came suddenly and struck you blind as well. . . . When the sun rose there as a white fog, very warm and clammy, and more blinding than the night. It did not shift or drive; it was just there, standing all around you like something solid. . . . We could see . . . just the steamer we were on, her outlines blurred as though she had been on the point of dissolving, and a misty strip of water, perhaps two feet broad, around her—and that was all. The rest of the world was

nowhere, as far as our eyes and ears were concerned. Just nowhere. Gone, disappeared; swept off without leaving a whisper or a shadow behind.' (16:101–2)

The blinding fog disorients the senses and reality seems to dissolve; the physicality of the world is called into question. This extraordinary experience occurs immediately before Marlow meets the heretical Kurtz, who will alter the tale-teller's conception of himself, humanity, and his culture. The disorienting fog is thus a sensory threshold that marks the boundary between the culturally familiar and the unfamiliar.

If the extraordinary sensation preceding altered awareness sometimes takes the form of anesthesia brought on by becalming, darkness, or fog, it just as often takes the form of synesthesia brought on by a tempestuous storm. In *The Nigger of the "Narcissus"* and *Typhoon*, Conrad describes the violence of the storms by piling on sensual details which evoke a synesthetic response in the reader. For the crew aboard the *Narcissus*, the sensual tumult brought on by the gale is reminiscent of De Quincey's hallucinatory experience in the Shrewsbury hotel:

> Now and then, for the fraction of an intolerable second, the ship, in the fiercer burst of a terrible uproar, remained on her side, vibrating and still, with a stillness more appalling than the wildest motion.... A fierce squall seemed to burst asunder the thick mass of sooty vapours; and above the wrack of torn clouds glimpses could be caught of the high moon rushing backwards with frightful speed over the sky, right into the wind's eye.... Soon the clouds closed up and the world again became a raging, blind darkness that howled, flinging at the lonely ship salt sprays and sleet. (23:54–55)

As if to emphasize the primacy of sensation as a way of knowing the phenomenal world, Conrad describes the storm itself as being an organ of sensation: the gale has an eye, and the clouds "close up" to leave the storm's victims in a state of confusion. In the last sentence of the passage, Conrad appeals to the oral, visual, aural, kinesthetic, and tactile senses, all of which are disturbed by the storm. The storm is imagined as an animistic force; the world becomes a darkness which howls and flings salty spray and frozen rain.

In *Typhoon*, the crew of the *Nan-Shan* experiences an identical disorientation. The storm

> seemed to explode all round the ship with an overpowering concussion and a rush of great waters. . . . The motion of the ship was extravagant. Her lurches had an appalling helplessness: she pitched as if taking a header into a void, and seemed to find a wall to hit every time. . . . The gale howled and scuffled about gigantically in the darkness, as though the entire world were one black gully. (20:40, 42–43)

The typhoon is even more literally disorienting to those aboard the *Nan-Shan* than to the men of the *Narcissus*. Though both crews are tossed about a good deal, the men in the hold of the *Nan-Shan* are virtually dismembered, reduced to "an inextricable confusion of heads and shoulders, naked soles kicking upwards, fists raised, tumbling backs, legs, pigtails, faces" (20:58), and the ship's crew members experience a "bodily fatigue" from the "mere holding on to existence within the excessive tumult" (20:52).

This tumultuous derangement of the senses exhausts the crew, but it also brings "a profound trouble to their souls" (20:47). Conrad here emphasizes the close connection between physical and psychical experience, the former largely determining the latter. This physical and psychic upheaval is met by attempts to reestablish order aboard ship. Wait's symbolic birth scene and MacWhirr's distribution of the crew's possessions are attempts to regain the equilibrium of ordinary perception and experience that characterizes the reality of the civilized world. In the former case, the crew tries to deliver Wait from his regressive, duty-shirking withdrawal, a dangerous form of chaos aboard ship. And the literal-minded MacWhirr tries to reestablish order after the storm by dispensing silver dollars.

The souls of Conrad's characters are troubled by chaotic and unfamiliar sensations which interrupt their habitual ways of seeing and thinking. Habitualized experience, the preoccupation with the reality of everyday duties, is a form of experience that many critics think Conrad strongly advocates.[6] Yet it is the figure who rejects the culturally familiar (or who is rejected by the culture) that Conrad portrays most sympathetically, in part, perhaps, because of his own cultural estrangement. His fiction is peopled with outcasts, exiles, hermits, and solitaries whose careers deviate sharply from what is culturally acceptable and who struggle desperately with a defamiliarized world which they, like the reader, do not know how to see.[7] The aim of Conrad's fiction, as we know from the preface to *The Nigger of the "Narcissus,"* is to inspire the reader to see and to understand something beyond what the ordinary, culturally competent individual sees and understands. To be sure, Conrad would be the last to say that this forsaking of duty and habitual perception is without danger. But his fascination with the heroic outcast who grapples with the unfamiliar is a testament to his preoccupation with, and attraction to, those individuals, even if they are ultimately destroyed by their venture.

In Conrad's fiction the characters most endangered by the unfamiliar are those outcasts who have functioned mindlessly in a culture which has deadened them to sensation, thought, and imagination. Carlier and Kayerts certainly fit this category. The journey they take away from their government offices, where all is routine, is a journey to their inexorable deaths:

> Dull as they were to the subtle influences of their surroundings, they felt themselves very much alone, when suddenly left unassisted to face the wilderness; a wilderness rendered more strange, more incomprehensible by the mysterious glimpses of the vigorous life it contained. They were two perfectly insignificant and incapable individuals, whose existence is only rendered possible through the high organization of civilized crowds. (8:89)

For the highly civilized individual who depends on the structure of society to organize his or her response to experience, the incomprehensibility of the wilderness is analogous to an extraordinary derangement of the senses. The crew of the *Nan-Shan* experience "a profound trouble to their souls" because the typhoon, which disturbs the order of the ship, isolates each of them. When the typhoon hits, each man is rendered an exile unto himself: "In an instant the men lost touch of each other. This is the disintegrating power of a great wind: it isolates one from one's kind" (20:40). The social outcast is likewise troubled in his soul as he confronts the unfamiliar sensations of the wilderness and an alien culture:

> But the contact with pure unmitigated savagery, with primitive nature and primitive man, brings sudden and profound trouble into the heart. To the sentiment of being alone of one's kind, to the clear perception of the loneliness of one's thoughts, of one's sensations—to the negation of the habitual, which is safe, there is added the affirmation of the unusual, which is dangerous; a suggestion of things vague, uncontrollable, and repulsive, whose discomposing intrusion excites the imagination and tries the civilized nerves of the foolish and the wise alike. (8:89)

The "negation of the habitual," or the disjoining of the cultural episteme, means the loss of a comfortable, a priori sense of reality. The reason Kayerts and Carlier fail, and fail quickly, is that they are incapable of responding to unfamiliar sensation.

The outcasts like Decoud and Willems, who are banished unwillingly from their civilizations and fail to comprehend unfamiliar sensations, also decline quickly. More capable outcasts, some of whom are self-exiled, find the unfamiliar equally intolerable and just as destructive. Lingard, Kurtz, and Lord Jim, for example, attempt to construct a society of their own in the wilderness, but their own civilization ultimately reclaims them. Even the hermit Heyst of *Victory,* who tries to cut himself off from nearly all human intercourse, cannot escape the "envoys of the outer world" (15:329).

Conrad concentrates on sharing with the reader the outcast's sensual experience; the reader sees what the exile sees. In virtually every case, Conrad's exile feels distanced from his own normal sensations; as if floating in a dream, he feels totally unconnected with the earth. This dreamlike suspension is usually hallucinatory in nature and signals a crossing of the shadow-line, a movement away from conventional perception. When Nostromo and Decoud leave the protection of the Sulaco jetty, for example, it is as if they were being "launched into space . . . [and] suspended in the air" (9:261). After Kurtz has succumbed to the "heavy, mute spell of the wilderness," Marlow describes him as one totally divorced from earthly experience: "He had kicked himself loose of the earth. Confound the man! he had kicked the very earth to pieces. He was alone, and I before him did not know whether I stood on the ground or floated in the air" (16:144). Kurtz's heretical alienation from civilization is described through a confusing and suspending of sense experience. This alienation induces a kind of cosmic vertigo in which the soul of the outcast is set adrift in space, no longer in touch with the earth which is the emblem of all that he once knew and was sure of. Like the less distinguished outcast Kayerts, who "kicks free of himself," Kurtz—and, to some degree, Marlow when in his presence—divests himself of his habitual restraints and perceptions as he disjoins the cultural episteme. This same sensation of suspension, used by Conrad to describe the moment when the outcast keenly senses his exile, is found in the hallucinatory passages in *Nostromo*. The Placid Gulf journey is likened to a dreamy state just before death: "Decoud shook himself, shuddered a bit, though the air that drifted past him was warm. He had the strangest sensation of his soul having just returned into his body from the circumambient darkness in which land, sea, sky, the mountains, and the rocks were as if they had not been" (9:262). Though for the moment Decoud is able to drift from his dream world back to the phenomenal world of water, land, and sky, once he is isolated on the Great Isabel, he again becomes "like a man in a dream" (9:301). "All his active sensations and feelings from as far back as he could remember seemed to him the maddest of dreams" (9:267). This hallucinatory state, brought on by sleeplessness and solitude, induces Decoud's fragmentary view of the universe.

The same hallucinatory dream state is used more extensively in conjunction with the theme of exile toward the middle and end of *An Outcast of the Islands*. Willems's decline in the novel is marked by progressively exaggerated sense perceptions, the first of which is a vision of his sudden death. As Willems lies drowsing in Aissa's arms, he has a vision of himself in exile:

> There was a long interval of silence. She stroked his head with gentle touches, and he lay dreamily, perfectly happy but for the annoyance of an indistinct vision of a well-known figure; a man going away from him and diminishing in a long perspective of fantastic trees, whose every leaf was an eye looking after that man, who walked away growing smaller, but never getting out of sight for all his steady progress. . . . There was something familiar about that figure. Why! Himself! . . . It had been half a dream; he had slumbered in her arms for a few seconds. Only the beginning of a dream—nothing more. (14:144–45)

Like Kurtz and Kayerts, who cut themselves off from the restraints of the civilized world and their cultural selves, Willems imagines himself out of his self. He envisions a double who is an outlaw, and who, like Leggatt in "The Secret Sharer," expresses the main character's social marginality: "It as like an evasion, like a prisoner breaking his parole—that thing slinking off stealthily while he slept" (14:145). Though clearly a metaphor for both exile and death—"If he had not woke up in time he would never have come back again from there; from whatever place he was going to" (14:145)—the hypnogogic vision that Willems has is transformed into the threatening reality of Aissa's blind but homicidal father. Willems recognizes Omar's face and the weapon clenched in his teeth, but he remains impassive before the ominous vision, his senses anesthetized: "The uneasy wonder and the obscure fear of that apparition . . . were drowned in the quietude of all his senses, as pain is drowned in the flood of drowsy serenity that follows upon a dose of opium" (14:147). Suggesting the neurotic paralysis that Conrad personally feared, Willems's paralysis is caused by a fear of the unfamiliar, the incomprehensible, the inscrutable: "It was not death that frightened him: it was the horror of bewildered life where he could understand nothing and nobody round him; where he could guide, control, comprehend nothing and no one—not even himself" (14:149).

Near the end of the novel, after Lingard's departure, Willems's dreamlike visions turn into nightmarish visions that are virtually identical to the alternating anesthesia and hyperesthesia of the opium addict. Willems's hellish visions culminate in an image of his own moral corruption; the very land overcomes him and hastens the disintegration already begun in his soul:

> He would be stretched upon the warm moisture of the ground, feeling nothing, seeing nothing, knowing nothing: he would lie stiff, passive, rotting slowly; while over him, under him, through him—unopposed, busy, hurried—the endless and minute throngs of insects, little shining monsters of repulsive shapes, with horns, with claws, with pincers, would swarm in streams, in rushes, in eager struggle for his body; would swarm countless, persistent, ferocious and greedy—till there would remain nothing but the white gleam of bleaching bones in the long grass. (14:331–32)

Once again, Conrad fuses the physical and psychical worlds; corporeal and moral corruption coalesce in a state of negated sensation, of "feeling nothing, knowing nothing."

The epistemology of *An Outcast*, like that in other Conrad novels, is heretical in that it offers a disoriented vision of the phenomenal world. The episteme of Conrad's work is characterized by a subversion of cultural perception brought on by the exile's estrangement from his native land. Like Coleridge's Mariner, Conrad's exiles experience a profound sensual disorientation—in fog, at night, in a typhoon—that separates the character from his culturally conditioned responses to experience.

While the heretical space of Conrad's journeys may be more conventionalized than that of other writers discussed in this study, his canon demonstrates the most consistent preoccupation in modern letters with the sensuous voyage of disorientation, a voyage that subverts the archetypal circular journey of the Christian episteme.

Six
Malcolm Lowry's Manichean Episteme: The Paradise of Despair

Inevitable destruction is . . . simply the teleological end of one series of possibilities; everything hopeful is equally possible.
—Malcolm Lowry, Letter to Derek Pethick

On the cardboard back of a notebook in which Malcolm Lowry kept notes for "The Forest Path to the Spring," the writer who produced what has been called the greatest religious novel of this century (Day 350) reflects on the relation of his beliefs to his art: "When I say [I have] come to grips I don't mean I merely passed beyond regrets & remorse to contrition. That is a great step in the soul, no doubt, but insufficient for a writer who wishing to write for God, yet has no priest, who believing, yet has no church, who is born religious, yet whose higher self dictates that he remain a heresiarch" (25:6, back cover).[1] Lowry's statement, which seems to articulate the acedia of the modern age, reveals a philosophical conflict that is apparent not only in Lowry's story but in virtually all of Lowry's works that were to comprise the cycle of fiction *The Voyage That Never Ends*. This conflict manifests itself in a Manichean, at times even schizophrenic, epistemology in which the mind of the novelist or a character simultaneously embraces or artistically balances visions of heaven and hell. Lowry, in his yearning for the integrated harmony of a beatific Eden and his intensely personal, mythopoeic vision of the hell of his own soul, is a romantic symbolist.

To understand the nature of this conflict in Lowry's art, we must first understand Lowry's work within the context of his projected cycle of novels provisionally titled *The Voyage That Never Ends*.[2] Lowry's plans for a masterwork akin to Proust's

Remembrances of Things Past, however, were formative, and thus the exact design of the cycle cannot be formulated with certainty. Lowry's letters and extensive notes on his "Work in Progress" reveal that he first envisioned a Dantesque trilogy and only later articulated a more ambitious plan. From Cuernavaca in January 1946, Lowry wrote to his London publisher, Jonathan Cape, that he had "conceived the idea of a trilogy entitled *The Voyage That Never Ends* . . . with the *Volcano* as the first, infernal part, a much amplified *Lunar Caustic* as the second, purgatorial part, and an enormous novel I was also working on called *In Ballast to the White Sea* . . . as the paradisal third part, the whole to concern the battering the human spirit takes . . . in its ascent toward its true purpose" (63). With the *Divine Comedy* as a structural antecedent and model, Lowry's trilogy is orthodoxically Christian in conception. But this concept, never realized, was transformed into a longer and, at least symbolically, less Christian journey in which the soul voyages continually in and out of various states of damnation and grace. Outlined in his "Work in Progress," the cycle was projected as follows:

THE VOYAGE THAT NEVER ENDS

THE ORDEAL OF SIGBJØRN WILDERNESS 1

UNTITLED SEA NOVEL [ULTRAMARINE]
LUNAR CAUSTIC

UNDER THE VOLCANO   The Centre

DARK AS THE GRAVE WHEREIN MY FRIEND IS
   LAID
ERIDANUS [OCTOBER FERRY TO GABRIOLA] } Trilogy
LA MORDIDA

THE ORDEAL OF SIGBJØRN WILDERNESS 2

(37: title page)

This longer cycle of novels that Lowry envisioned still showed a general movement from disintegration to reintegration—the manuscript version of "The Ordeal of Sigbjørn Wilderness" is the story of a novelist who falls from a pier, breaks his back, and hallucinates during his stay in hospital, and "The Ordeal of Sigbjørn Wilderness 2" was to recount his physical and spiritual recovery—but the works Lowry completed during his lifetime do not show such a neat progressive pattern. All of Lowry's mature fiction, even the hellish *Lunar Caustic*[3] and the halcyon "The Forest Path to the Spring," involves what Lowry called an "ingress and egress" of the soul that is eternally changing, eternally moving between two extremes.

Caught between two conflicting visions of reality, Lowry was unable to resolve in his own mind a dominant perceiving self, either in his own life or in his fiction. This psychological schizophrenia does not, however, translate into an art that is tentative in conception but rather into fiction that acknowledges the richness and complexity of possible artistic responses to the human and physical universe. *The Voyage That Never Ends* was thus conceived as a journey whose teleology is obscured by the presence of competing constructive and destructive epistemologies, one projecting a harmonious vision of the individual and nature under what Lowry terms the celestial circuits and the other a disintegration of man and nature under the disjoining heavenly circuits. Sherrill Grace has recognized this aspect of Lowry's work as the

> inescapable presence throughout of an encyclopaedic perceiving consciousness. Lowry's unifying principle of repetition is nowhere more obvious . . . than in the repeated narrative pattern of withdrawal and return, and whether the movement of withdrawal from reality occurs on an epistemological or a psychological level, or more simply on the level of ordinary personal relationship, it is always a negative state characterized by narrative and stylistic stasis and by a character's emotional, spiritual, or physical death. Return from this state, like the flow of the tides, brings movement, clarity, balance and joy—'as by a miracle.' (18–19)

Lowry's Manichean epistemology is apparent in both the perception of Lowry's narrators and characters as well as the implied literary epistemology of the writer himself and manifests itself in the language, images, and structure of his works.

The Linguistic Basis of Lowry's Episteme

Writing in the literary aftermath of Joyce's *Portrait* and *Ulysses,* Lowry was attentive to the close relationship between language, questions of epistemology, and fictional reality. In its most rudimentary form, this interconnection is apparent in Lowry's love of juxtaposing lexical opposites. His oxymoronic combinations most frequently yoke the concepts of heaven and hell. This is most apparent in *Under the Volcano* when the Consul describes his own garden and the Mexican landscape as possessing an "infernal beauty" (144). The various drafts of *Volcano* reveal constant experimentation with such combinations as "obscene beauty" (Lowry Papers 8:5, 137) and "desolate fecundity" (10:14, 1). The paradoxical word play reflects the Consul's "gruesome gaiety" (354), the fact that he "love[s] hell" (314). The joining of opposites is also evident in the many multilingual puns in which words with positive connotations are replaced by those having negative connotations. At the Salon Ofelia in chapter 10 of *Volcano,* for instance, the Consul and company order the "spectral [for special] chicken of the house" (291). Both kinds of lexical paradox reflect in miniature the schizophrenic episteme that is further expressed in Lowry's style and word play and themes.

The language of Lowry's fictional style reflects both a creative and destructive epistemology. In much of Lowry's fiction, the creative episteme is projected by the central female figure and is characterized by an affirmation of beautiful images in the world. Primrose Wilderness in *Dark As the Grave Wherein My Friend Is Laid* is an example: "She was a person whose creative perception was simply that of creative life and living, not a writer, but a person who loves life, who expresses her creative life in the *living* of life" (202). The world view of Primrose, like that of Yvonne in *Volcano,* is intimately associated with Lowry's "Columbian Eden,"[4] the locale that Lowry describes in his most lyrical and most beautiful prose. Such lyric passages occur in *Volcano,* in the "Eridanus" passages in *October Ferry to Gabriola,* and throughout much of "The Forest Path to the Spring," which Lowry dedicated to his second wife. These beautiful passages, with their images of natural abundance, growth, harmony, and equilibrium, reflect the novelist's constructive projection of an ideal world. "The Forest Path" begins with descriptions of lyric beauty and calm:

> At dusk, every evening, I used to go through the forest to the spring for water.
>
> The way that led to the spring from our cabin was a path wandering along the bank of the inlet through snowberry and thimbleberry and shallon bushes, with the sea below you on the right, and the shingled roofs of the houses, all built down on the beach beneath round the little crescent of the bay. . . .
>
> Beyond, going toward the spring, through the trees, range beyond celestial range, crowded the mountains, snow-peaked for most of the year. At dusk they were violet, and frequently they looked on fire, the white fire of the mist. Sometimes in the early mornings this mist looked like a huge family wash, the property of Titans, hanging out to dry between the folds of their lower hills. At other times all was chaos, and Valkyries of storm-drift drove across them out of the ever reclouding heavens. (Lowry 1961, 215)

The balance, poise, and rhythm of Lowry's prose reflects an edenic sense of place, "that marvelous region of wilderness known to the Indians as Paradise" (219). On the one hand, Lowry's description simply conveys his spiritual affection for the environs of Burrard Inlet where he and Margerie lived in a squatter's hut, but within the context of Lowry's entire canon the passages describing Eridanus convey a creative, beatific vision. For Lowry, a direct literary descendent of the English romantics, mental and physical landscapes coalesce in a vision projected by the creative mind of the artist.

Such creative projections reside in more than the lyrical beauty of his prose. Mental creativity is also associated with the Consul's verbal puns whose private linguistic world is also part of Lowry's constructive episteme. Often Lowry's comedy in *Volcano* is at a high point in these moments of linguistic play:

> '—Hullo-hullo-look-who-comes-hullo-my-little-snake-in-the-grass-my-little-anguish-in-herba—' the Consul at this moment greeted Mr. Quincey's cat, momentarily forgetting its owner again as the grey, meditative animal, with a tail so long it trailed on the ground, came stalking through the zinnias: he stooped, patting his thighs—'hello-pussy-my-little-Priapusspuss-my-little-Oedipusspusspuss,' and the cat, recognizing a friend and uttering a cry of pleasure, wound through the fence and rubbed against the Consul's legs, purring. 'My little Xicotancatl.' The Consul stood up. He gave two short whistles while below him the cat's ears twirled. 'She thinks I'm a tree with a bird in it,' he added. (134)

In this particular instance, the Consul's friendly banter, though tending toward the solipsistic, is a constructive projection of a reality that encompasses the sensual world of a cat in a garden, the human mythology of the Greek, Christian, and Mexican cultures, and the neologistic mind of the Consul. In other instances in Lowry's fiction, the projective vision of the Consul is entirely internalized, though no less creative:

> The Consul's voice came from far away. He was aware of vertigo; closing his eyes wearily he took hold of the fence to steady himself. Mr. Quincey's words knocked on his consciousness—or someone actually was knocking on a door—fell away, then knocked again, louder. Old De Quincey; the knocking on the gate in Macbeth. Knock knock: who's there? Cat. Cat who? Catastrophe. Catastrophe who? Catastrophysicist. What is it you, my

little popocat? Just wait an eternity till Jacques and I have finished murdering sleep! Katabasis to cat abysses. Cathartes atratus . . . (136)

The sense of vertigo—which, in Lowry's fiction, indicates his constructive epistemology—triggers the Consul's highly associative, verbal imagination. These linguistic flights of imagination test the reader's knowledge of literature and myth as well as one's understanding of the Consul's temperament and the complexity of his mind.

While such associative word play frequently conveys the positive force of human consciousness and understanding, there are as many times when the language reflects a destructive episteme. In these instances, language itself is responsible for the disintegration of certain knowledge and meaning, as in the Consul's mistranslation of

¿LE GUSTA ESTE JARDÍN

QUE ES SUYO?

¡EVITE QUE SUS HIJOS LO DESTRUYAN![5]

or Dr. Vigil's unidiomatic malapropism "Throw away your mind." This latter expression, occurring as it does in the opening conversation between M. Laruelle and Dr. Vigil in the first chapter of the novel, establishes the epistemological uncertainty of *Under the Volcano* and anticipates the numerous extended conversations in which language simultaneously creates and destroys meaning in the novel.[6] Perhaps the most poignant example of this linguistic uncertainty is the conversation between the Consul and Señora Gregorio:

> Señora Gregorio took his hand and held it. 'Life changes, you know,' she said, gazing at him intently. 'You can never drink of it. I think I see you with your esposa again soon. I see you laughing together in some kernice place where you laugh.' She smiled. 'Far away. In some kernice place where all those troubles you har now will har—' The Consul started: what was Señora Gregorio saying? 'Adiós,' she added in Spanish. 'I have

no house only a shadow. But whenever you are in need of a shadow, my shadow is yours.'
'Thank you.'
'Sank you.'
'Not sank you, Señora Gregorio, thank you.'
'Sank you.' (229–30)

The confusion of drink/think, life/laugh, kernice/nice, sank/thank, shadow/chateau are verbally playful constructions yet destructive of understanding. Furthermore, the linguistic misstatements of such characters as Dr. Vigil, Señora Gregorio, and Cervantes at the Salon Ofelia mirror on a linguistic level the failure of communication between the Consul and Yvonne, as we will see later.

The potential for language to disorient the reader by reflecting a divided episteme is perhaps clearest in Lowry's "Through the Panama," a lengthy short story in *Hear Us O Lord from Heaven Thy Dwelling Place*. This self-conscious literary text is in the form of a diary, kept by a writer traveling from Vancouver, British Columbia, to Europe via the Panama Canal. While the story itself is experimental and perhaps imperfect, it illustrates in exaggerated form a formal linguistic disorientation like that in Coleridge's "The Ancient Mariner." Lowry adapts Coleridge's use of glosses to demonstrate the diary author's schizophrenic perceptions and social disorientation. The marginal glosses of Sigbjørn Wilderness include both original, self-reflexive text and direct quotes from Coleridge and Helen Nicolay's *Bridge of Water,* an early twentieth-century history of the building of the Panama Canal. The glosses sometimes offer ironic commentary but more often create a sense of verbal pastiche. The competing texts present divergent perspectives that reflect the physical disorientation of ship travel and the psychological disorientation of the diarist who is presumably intoxicated during much of the passage. This technique, more obviously than the multilingual puns and miscommunications in *Volcano,* shows Lowry's conscious adaptation of Coleridge's use of linguistic disorientation to convey estrangement from the cultural episteme.

The Imagery of Disorientation: Vertiginous and Entropic Extremes

The sense of vertiginous motion that pervades Lowry's work reflects the "whirling cerebral chaos" experienced by many of Lowry's protagonists. While this sense of whirling is often associated with disorientation in his characters, for Lowry vertiginous motion is also intimately associated with the life force inherent in the "madly revolving world" and the celestial spheres. The images of gyration, spiraling, wheeling, and whirling are for Lowry kinetic forces that animate the universe. Conversely, the idea of entropy in Lowry's work is conveyed by images of destruction: fragmentation, collapse, dispersal, inertia, and cessation. It would be convenient if Lowry's attitude toward these sensate extremes were consistent and if the entropic images of stasis or the vertiginous images of kinetic flux were presented consistently and in isolation from each other. But this is not the case. Lowry's characters vacillate between a longing for the stasis of death and an intense sense of the joyful if chaotic flux of an animistic world. Most of Lowry's protagonists envision a world which combines constructive and destructive experiences, and his works reveal a schizophrenic view of reality.

The narrator of an unpublished version of *Lunar Caustic*, "Swinging the Maelstrom," identifies his own psychological schizophrenia, claiming "he must be at least two persons drinking: the first, to whom the whole business of living at all was abhorrent, drank obscurely and mostly out of a bottle, whereas the second, gregarious and cheerful, drank at the bar" (Lowry's Papers 22:7, 2). In the published version, edited by Earl Birney and Margerie Lowry, this schizophrenia is expressed in the narrator's ontological confusion as he alternately identifies himself as a ship and a human with the respective names of S. S. Lawhill and Bill Plantagenet (13). So intensely was Lowry engaged in creating the schizophrenic perception of characters that, in notes to himself or his publisher, he asserts that the form of his work began to reflect its content: a "schizophrenia—not in the characters but within the story—arises" (22:5, 36B). While Lowry was probably interested in schizophrenia as a result of his commitment to the psychiatric wing of Bellevue Hospital, he was also fascinated with the idea of schizophrenia as the product of mystical perception. Lowry's esoteric interests led him to the writings of P. D. Ouspensky,[7] whose works on mysticism and sensationalism Lowry read with excitement (Letters 26). Lowry might have found Ouspensky's comments on Nietzsche's superman attractive, for they describe a divided perceiving self:

> Man is pre-eminently a transitional form, constant only in his contradictions and inconstancy—moving, becoming, changing under our eyes. . . .
> So many and opposing principles struggle in man that a harmonious coordination of them is quite impossible. . . . Man is a little universe. In him proceed continual death and continual birth, the incessant swallowing of one being by another, the devouring of the weaker by the stronger, evolution and degeneration, growing and dying out. Man has within him everything from mineral to God. And the desire of God in man, that is, the directing forces of his spirit, conscious of its unity with the infinite consciousness of the universe, cannot be in harmony with the inertia of a stone, with the inclination of particles for crystallization. . . .
> And the more man develops inwardly, the more strongly he begins to feel the different sides of his soul simultaneously. (Ouspensky 1971, 105)

Ouspensky's belief in the simultaneous existence of godlike creative powers and a tendency toward inertia in humans has much in common with Lowry's sense of a divided self that is half creative and half self-destructive. Ouspensky himself identified such a schizophrenic state in a chapter called "Experimental Mysticism" in *A New Model of the Universe*. He speaks of "a sensation of strange duality in myself. . . . When this change came I found myself in a world entirely new and entirely unknown to me, which had nothing in common with the world in which we live, still less with the world which we assume to be the continuation of our world in the direction of the unknown" (277). Ouspensky's mystical experiments seem designed to disjoin the self from its social identity and the cultural episteme. In his fiction, Lowry constantly experimented with narrators and protagonists who have a divided state of mind and whose epistemological processes are alternately constructive and destructive.

The imagery that expresses this schizophrenic epistemology is developed with the most complexity and richness in *Under the Volcano,* but it can be examined in its purest form in shorter works such as *Ultramarine* and *Lunar Caustic.* Even in his earliest work, Lowry displays his preoccupation with extraordinary sense perception which was so crucial in his epistemology. Under the influence of both alcohol and such sea writers as Joseph Conrad, Conrad Aiken, Jack London, Richard H. Dana, and Nordahl Grieg, Lowry begins his career writing about the sense disorientation associated with intoxication and sailing the sea. His first novel, *Ultramarine,* which he wrote while a student at Cambridge, is a virtual catalogue of hyperesthetic sensations which he collected during his six-month voyage as a deck hand on the *SS Pyrrhus.* The young hero in *Ultramarine* boards ship "having been blown through [a] six weeks' engulfing darkness" (15) and notes the hawkers who "surge on to the ship" and the stevedores who "swing in on the derricks" (16). He stares at birds perched atop the "swaying mainmasthead" (18) and feels the "joyous derangement of the boundless waste" (24). During working hours he dodges "swinging cargo" (31) and during off hours or shore leave enjoys the "eternal vortex of youth" (37). The opening pages of the novel develop patterns of imagery that anticipate Dana Hilliot's first drunk worthy of a sailor, an experience described as a complex of vertiginous and entropic extremes. Supine and intoxicated on his bunk aboard the *Oedipus Tyrannus,* Dana feels the world whirling around him until objects explode and spin off into space like dispersing celestial bodies:

> Then he lay down flat on his back. He began slowly to go to sleep, gliding, as it were, down a steep incline. . . . Electric lights swam past. Gas jets, crocus-coloured, steadily flared and whirred. The shouts and cries of the market rose and fell about them like the breathing of a monster. Above, the moon soared and galloped through a dark, tempestuous sky. All at once, every lamp in the street exploded, their globes flew out, darted into the sky, and the street become alive with eyes, . . . eyes which wavered, and spread, and, diminishing rapidly, were catapulted east and west. (43–44)

This hypnagogic vision is an early example of Lowry's dual epistemology which is simultaneously constructive and destructive. The episode is characterized by the contradictory states of static calm as Dana lies on his back and vertiginous chaos as he imagines a disordered cosmos exploding before his eyes.

Some two years after the publication of *Ultramarine,* Lowry was admitted to Bellevue Hospital in New York for psychiatric observation and treatment (Day 196). His stay of two to three weeks, like his voyage on the *Pyrrhus,* furnished him with material for his writing. And, like his experience at sea, his incipient alcoholism and confinement at Bellevue increased his fascination with sensual disorientation and altered states of mind. The novella that resulted, *Lunar Caustic,* occupied his attention from the summer of 1935 until its publication in the *Paris Review* in 1953, and even after that. We can only speculate why the work preoccupied Lowry as much as it did and why the various versions he wrote—"The Last Address," "Swinging the Maelstrom," and finally *Lunar Caustic*—express such different psychological outlooks, but it seems likely that Lowry was trying to establish an imagistic vocabulary that would express his deeply divided epistemology.

The final work, about schizophrenia, reflects its subject in the multiple visions it presents. Images of life and death, heaven and hell, motion and stasis are yoked together. In *Lunar Caustic* Plantagenet, the central character, imagines he is "lying in the propeller shaft" (14) of the mental ward that vertiginously whirls around him, and yet the sense of whirling finally ends in a feeling of entropic chaos and collapse, of all things are moving toward a state of inertia. Plantagenet likens this paradoxical combination to a descent into the maelstrom reminiscent of Poe:

> Plantagenet suspected he was the only one who was frightened; nor was he frightened now so much by . . . the shadows, which partook of the familiarity of his delirium. . . . He had the curious feeling that he had made a sort of descent into the maelstrom, a maelstrom terrifying for the last reason one might have expected: that there was about it sometimes just this loathsome, patient calm. (37)

This curious yoking of disparate sensations is not accidental or anomalous but rather establishes a pattern of imagery carried throughout the work. The most conscious use of such imagery occurs when Plantagenet describes the Rimbaudian stories told by one of the patients named Garry, a young man who is arrested in his mental and emotional development but whose imaginative faculties are undiminished. Impatient with the unimaginative doctor, Plantagenet scolds, "'Don't you see its the same kind of thing [as Rimbaud]? *Mêlant aux fleurs des yeux des panthères*—etc. And all his stories about things collapsing, falling apart.'" This feeling of collapse is directly associated with the sensation of personal vertigo: "'It extends to the *world*—do I have to shriek at you?—that sense of decay, the necessity of blasting away the past, the feeling of *vertige*'" (57). Both Garry and Plantagenet feel a need to subvert the cultural episteme, to blast away the past, which is accomplished by projecting a vision of the universe as whirling itself into a chaos that explodes and disperses leaving behind calm and stillness.

These images of hyperesthetic sense perception are critical to an understanding of Lowry's fictional world, for the vertiginous and entropic forces express the beatific and demonic animism of Lowry's Manichean episteme. The animism of Lowry's fiction is more than mere anthropomorphizing; rather, Lowry assumes that the entire physical universe is endowed with spiritual life that can be beatific or demonic. Lowry articulates his animistic world view most clearly in expository passages in *October Ferry to Gabriola,* the novel Lowry was working on when he died. The autobiographical protagonist maintains that all men are "animists at heart" and seek to love the world's objects as if they are "sentient thing[s]" (73–74). Such objects, in Lowry's fiction acquire a life, a character, even a spiritual intellect of their own. In the chapter of *October Ferry* titled "The Element Follows You Around, Sir!," which illustrates the benign and threatening aspects of Lowry's animism, Ethan Llewelyn describes his own consciousness as bringing the phenomenal world to life: "It was as if the subjective world within . . . had somehow turned itself inside out: as if the objective world without had itself caught a sort of hysteria" (115–16). This animistic transferal of life gives phenomena a totally independent existence: "Phenomena went galloping and gambolling over the whole countryside, though now and then . . . the 'intelligence' expressed itself almost benignly" (119). Because it is the perceiver who endows the phenomenal world with life, these animistic forces are often projections of the perceiver's deepest fears about the self or the threatening world beyond the self. Ethan, the protagonist of *October Ferry,* thus conceives of nature as "having a kind of nervous breakdown" (121), most apparent during the fury of electrical storms, which end with an entropic disintegration of the vertiginous movements of the cosmos. Ethan witnesses "huge aerial battles above the lake" which become a "kind of celestial disorder of the kinaesthesia" (120). Lowry's protaxis, a psychological disorder in which an individual cannot distinguish himself from the universe (Day 69), extends to his protagonists whose psychological conflicts are reflected in constructive perceptions of beauty in the world and destructive perceptions of a threatening phenomenal world.

At one extreme in Lowry's episteme is "The Forest Path to the Spring," the final story of *Hear Us O Lord from Heaven Thy Dwelling Place.* A beatific animism pervades the edenic landscape of this great lyrical confession. Although the beatific animism of "Eridanus," as Lowry called it, is implicit in the lovingly detailed descriptions of nature in the story, it is stated thematically in a description of the lighthouse on Burrard Inlet in British Columbia:

> It was a whitewashed concrete structure, thin as a match, like a magic lighthouse, without a keeper, but oddly like a human being itself, standing lonely on its cairn with its ruby lamp for a head and its generator strapped to its back like a pack; wild roses in early summer blew on the bank beside it, and when the evening star came out, sure enough, it began its beneficent signaling too. (218)

Unlike the Farolito ("the lighthouse that invites the storm") of *Under the Volcano*, the lighthouse at Eridanus is a symbol of the dominant episteme of the story. Like the lighthouse, the story is a beautiful projection of edenic order on earth, of life in harmony with the "beneficent signaling" of the whirling heavens.

As in nearly all of Lowry's work, however, even in this most purely beatific piece, there is a counterpoint of demonic animism: "the red votive candle of the burning oil wastes flickering ceaselessly all night before the gleaming open cathedral of the oil refinery" (226). To be sure, the refinery is on a distant shoreline across the inlet on the Vancouver side, but it is always there, belching smoke by day, demonically burning by night, and always exhibiting its poignantly unfinished advertisement that reads HELL instead of SHELL (256). The refinery, a symbol of the destructiveness of the war effort, counterbalances the beneficent force of the lighthouse. The destructive epistemology represented by the refinery is clearly subordinate in the story but can, at any time, color the mental lives of the narrator and his wife:

> And at night, when we opened the window, from the lamps within our shadows were projected out to sea, on the fog, against the night, and sometimes they were huge, menacing. One night coming across the porch

> from the woodshed with a lantern in one hand and a load of wood under the other arm, I saw my shadow, gigantic, the logs of wood as big as a coffin, and this shadow seemed for a moment the glowering embodiment of all that threatened us; yes, even a projection of the dark chaotic side of myself, my ferocious destructive ignorance. (233)

In this passage, the beneficent signaling of the lighthouse has been replaced by a spectral projection of "destructive ignorance." Thus, while a constructive epistemology dominates in "The Forest Path," a demonic, destructive epistemology is still present. Lowry's world view is Manichean and thus Eridanus is both "the River of Death and the River of Life" (226).

If benign, or beatific, animism dominates the lyrical "Forest Path," demonic animism prevails in *Lunar Caustic*. But again both poles of Lowry's epistemology are present. The following two paragraphs provide an example of the juxtaposition of these disparate world views:

> Every so often, when a ship passed, there would be a curious mass movement towards the barred windows, a surging whose source was in the breasts of the mad seamen and firemen there, but to which all were tributary: even those whose heads had been bowed for days rose at this stirring, their bodies shaking as though roused suddenly from nightmare or from the dead, while their lips would burst with sound, partly a cheer and partly a wailing shriek, like some cry of the imprisoned spirit of New York itself, that spirit haunting the abyss between Europe and America and brooding like futurity over the Western Ocean. The eyes of all would watch the ship with a strange, hungry supplication.
> But more often when a ship went by or backed out from the docks opposite and swung around to steam towards the open sea, there was dead silence in the ward and a strange foreboding as though all hope were sailing with the tide. (13)

In these two paragraphs we see the tension between two opposing forces: in the first a life force surging, stirring, shaking, rousing, and bursting, in the second "dead silence." The patients respond to the ships as if they possessed different souls, one benign, which animates the men, the other demonic, provoking thoughts of death.

Of course the animism in *Lunar Caustic,* because it is the projection of the delirious mind of the alcoholic Plantagenet, is most often threatening and demonic. "The periodic, shuddering metamorphoses his mind projected upon almost every object" (21) creates a landscape in which "Nature herself is shot through with jitteriness" (26). New York City is transformed into a "mighty force" that "groans and roars above, around, below [Plantangenet]. . . . A bridge strides over the river. Signs nod past him" (9). "A smudged gasworks crouched like something that could spring" (12). Lowry's setting is similar to the supernatural landscape projected by Coleridge's Ancient Mariner but is translated into modern urban terms:

> Where were all the good honest ships tonight, [Plantagenet] wondered, bound for all over the world? Lately it had seemed to him they passed more rarely. Only nightmare ships were left in this stream. All at once, watching the strange traffic upon it, he fancied that the East River was as delirious, as haunted as the minds that brooded over it, it was a mad river of grotesque mastless steamers, of flat barges slipping along silent as water snakes. (65)

A projection of mental instability, this demonic landscape is envisioned by the story-teller Garry as a landscape of death and destruction: "This world of the river was one where everything was uncompleted while functioning in degeneration, from which as from Garry's barge, the image of their own shattered or unformed souls was cast back at them" (65).

Though the fictional worlds of "The Forest Path" and *Lunar Caustic* may seem to be entirely different, they are in fact the product of the same dualistic world view. Whether a constructive or destructive episteme dominates, the opposing view is never entirely denied but is always waiting to reassert itself with a shift in schizophrenic perception. The same may be said of Lowry's entire canon. While one side of his epistemology may dominate a particular work, there is always another work that embodies the other side. Lowry's work as a whole thus exhibits a Manichean balance between benign and demonic world views.

Under the Volcano: *The Structure of Disorientation*

In Lowry's famous thirty-one page letter to his publisher Jonathan Cape, in which he defends *Under the Volcano* against the editorial demand to cut and revise, Lowry describes the structure of his masterpiece, defining the relation of individual parts to the whole: "That which may seem inorganic in itself might prove right in terms of the whole churrigueresque structure I conceived and which I hope may begin soon to loom out of the fog for you like Borda's horrible-beautiful cathedral in Taxco" (61). This metaphorical description of the baroque structure of his novel was not flippant. Lowry spent two weeks writing his letter, and his papers as well as his other works (e.g., *Dark As the Grave,* 62) show that Borda's cathedral and its "churrigueresque" structure preoccupied him during and immediately after the writing of *Under the Volcano.* Like the baroque architecture of the "horrible-beautiful" cathedral, Lowry's work appears excessive and "horrible" in detail, but each individual arabesque contributes to the organic beauty of the whole. Lowry's description of the structure of his novel as "horrible-beautiful" again suggests his dualistic episteme: the disposition of the vertiginous and entropic images give the novel its "horrible-beautiful" structure that is simultaneously balanced and disorienting. The overall structure of the novel is thus based upon competing aesthetic sensations of harmony, balance, and poise on the one hand, and discord, imbalance, and tension on the other.

Lowry's Manichean episteme is evident in the images of vertigo and entropy that dominate the Consul's alcohol-inspired world view in *Under the Volcano*. As Max-Pol Fouchet observes, "*L'alcool, pour* [the Consul] *n'est pas un vice, mais une passion de l'âme, un moyen de la connaissance. L'éthylisme de Geoffrey atteint ce dérèglement des sens, par lequel, aux terms de Rimbaud, on se fait voyant*" (26). [Alcohol, for the Consul, is not a vice but a passion of the soul, a medium of knowledge. The chronic intoxication of Geoffrey attains to a derangement of the senses, by which, in Rimbaud's terms, one becomes a seer.] In Lowry's words, this way of knowing and writing approaches a "disorder of the kinaesthesia" (*Letters* 312) in which the Consul's "whirling cerebral chaos" (308) produces and corresponds to the "madly revolving world" (194). The Consul's sense derangement, like the pleasures and pains of opium, can be either benign or demonic. In the case of his fateful ride on the "*Máquina Infernal*," or Ferris wheel, the sense disorientation and resulting vertigo are strictly associated with the Consul's intense and self-inflicted suffering which inexorably leads to his death. On the other hand, the Consul's sense of the world whirling around him, even when he is so near his tragic end, is comically translated into a joke whose irony is missed by the Mexican policeman. Making fun of his own condition, the Consul observes with tragic insight, "'I learn that the world goes round so I am waiting here for my house to pass by'" (355). This paradoxical combination of spinning and standing still is common in the novel. The Consul experiences an entropic inertia as he perceives the world to be hurtling vertiginously around him.

The Consul also has an entropic sense of the collapse or dissemination of self and the phenomenal world. Like Yvonne, who experiences a "recurrent nightmare of things collapsing" (260), the Consul hears the remote sound of "subterranean collapse" (337). At one point the Consul feels he is literally disintegrating into the otherness of the physical universe: "He had peered out at the garden, and it was as though bits of his eyelids had broken off and were flittering and jittering before him, turning into nervous shapes and shadows, jumping to the guilty chattering in his mind" (144–45). The sense of personal fragmentation and disintegration is equally apparent in the Consul's metaphor of himself as a tower of bottles, which topple, shattering his identity:

> Suddenly he saw them, the bottles of aguardiente, of anís, or jarez, of Highland Queen, the glasses, a babel of glasses—towering, . . . built to the sky, then falling, the glasses toppling and crashing, falling downhill from the Generalife Gardens, the bottles breaking, bottles of Oporto, tinto, blanco, bottles of Pernod, Oxygènée, absinthe, bottles smashing, bottles cast aside, falling with a thud on the ground in parks, under benches, beds, cinema seats, hidden in drawers at Consulates, bottles of Calvados dropped and broken, or bursting into smithereens, tossed into garbage heaps, flung into the sea, the Mediterranean, the Caspian, the Caribbean, bottles floating in the ocean, . . . bottles, bottles, bottles, and glasses, glasses, glasses, of bitter, of Dubonnet, of Falstaff, Rye, Johnny Walker, Vieux Whiskey blanc Canadien, the apéritifs, the digestifs, the demis, the dobles, the noch ein Herr Obers, the et glas Araks, the tusen taks, the bottles, the bottles, the beautiful bottles of tequila. . . . The Consul sat very still. His conscience sounded muffled with the roar of water. . . . How indeed could he hope to find himself, to begin again, when, somewhere, perhaps in one of those lost or broken bottles, in one of those glasses, lay, forever, the solitary clue to his identity? (292–93)

The Consul's concept of self and of his drinking coalesce in a catalogue of deranging elixirs, and the disintegration of self, a kind of willed self-destruction, is conveyed by the image of crashing and fragmenting booze bottles, which are emblems of his identity.

The same entropic forces that cause the fragmentation and dissemination of self are responsible for the failure of communication between the Consul and Yvonne, a failure which precipitates the tragedy of the novel. There are numerous instances where information fails to be communicated physically between the Consul and Yvonne: Yvonne's fateful postcard that wanders abroad for a year before reaching the Consul; the letter from the Consul to Yvonne that M. Laruelle finds, a year after their deaths, in the Consul's book of Elizabethan plays; and, most importantly, the letters from Yvonne to the Consul that were either misaddressed or never answered. To the very end, the Consul cannot understand these letters: "The Consul read this sentence over and over again, the same sentence, the same letter, all of the letters vain as those arriving on shipboard in port for one lost at sea, because he found some difficulty in focussing, the words kept blurring and dissembling, his own name staring out at him." Here, the Consul's distorted perception, his self-destruction, and the loss of meaning are directly connected. In the same way that bits of the Consul's eyelids, in an earlier scene, break off and seem to merge with the landscape, language itself, by the end of the novel, has begun to disintegrate and communication comes to an entropic standstill: "But the mescal had brought him in touch with his situation again to the extent that he did not now need to comprehend any meaning in the words beyond their abject confirmation of his own lostness, his own fruitless selfish ruin, now perhaps finally self-imposed, his brain . . . at an agonized standstill" (345).

The competing images of vertigo and entropy in the *Volcano* are part of the novel's baroque texture, which is organized by what David Hayman, in a study of *Finnegans Wake,* has termed a nodal structure:

> The key element . . . is the "prime node" or apex of the "nodal system," a passage where some act, activity, personal trait, allusion, theme, etc. surfaces for its clearest statement in the text, is made manifest, so to speak, and in the process brings together and crystallizes an otherwise scattered body of related material. This prime node is the generative center for lesser and generally less transparent passages devoted to its elaboration or expansion and strategically located in the text. The latter

are reinforced by more numerous but briefer allusions to one or more of its attributes. As the units diminish in size, their distribution becomes increasingly, though never truly, random. Taken together, all of these components constitute a single nodal system though on occasion one prime node may generate more than one system and though such systems tend to be interrelated. (136)

Hayman argues that a work of fiction can thus have a rather clearly ordered superstructure and a less obvious organization (or infrastructure) on the textual level. While the superstructure of *Volcano* is straightforward—twelve chapters suggests the number of waking hours in a day or the number of months in a year, and the number has other cabalistic and numerological associations—the infrastructure of the novel is more complex. It is governed by a primary node that serves as the center of the novel, structuring narrative as well as creating theme and metaphor. In a text like the *Volcano* which often avoids the traditional patterns of sequential narration, the primary node gives the novel formal coherence by ramifying into minor nodes of significance and clusters of motifs which give the work its baroque texture. Lowry clearly had this technique in mind when he cites in his famous letter to Jonathan Cape the baroque quality of his fiction: each literary arabesque is a minor node that relates to the central node which determines the major themes of the novel.

The central node in *Under the Volcano* is the luminous wheel, representing, in Lowry's words, not only "the Ferris wheel in the square, but . . . if you like, also many other things: it is Buddha's wheel of the law, . . . it is eternity, it is the instrument of the eternal recurrence, the eternal return, and it is the form of the book; or superficially it can be seen simply in an obvious movie sense as the wheel of time whirling backwards until we have reached the year before and Chapter II" (*Letters* 70–71). The major event involving the luminous wheel is the Consul's fateful Ferris wheel ride which occurs close to the midpoint of the novel. While the central location of this episode suggests its importance, the node of the luminous wheel is also the source of most of the major themes, images, and recurring details in the novel.

The Consul's experiences with the *"Máquina Infernal"* (221), or infernal machine, as the Ferris wheel is called, produces the Consul's most violent, most vertiginous derangement of the senses, and it is this disorientation that causes his identity, in the form of his passport, to be stripped from him, an event that is both the literal cause and a symbol of his destruction. The luminous wheel is thus a demonic force that gives rise to imagery, themes, and symbols associated with hell, for example, the Hotel della Selva, suggesting Dante's wood (Cross 29), Laruelle's circuitous descent into Quauhnahuac (23), the descent of the bus into Tomalín (252), the Farolito as "Infierno" (147), young Geoffrey Firmin's "Hell Bunker" (20), and the older Consul's assertion that he loves hell (314). Since the central node of the luminous wheel is also meant to be a crucifixion scene, it connects the Consul's suffering with his ultimate destination, the barranca. Referring to the mythic formation of the ravine, Laruelle relates that "when Christ was being crucified, so ran the sea-borne, hieratic legend, the earth had opened all through this country" (15). Thus, by extension, the luminous wheel which gives rise to the demonic motifs of the inferno and the abyss of the barranca also gives rise to the related motifs of the Farolito, Parián, and pariah dogs, all nodal motifs in their own right.

As a counterbalance to these demonic motifs, the luminous wheel also generates the major beneficent force in the novel, the millwheel, which is associated with a constructive vision of cosmic harmony. References to the "the luminous wheel of this gallaxy" (322), "millwheel reflections of sunlight on water" (270, 112), and "the vast spokes of the wheel whirling across the bay" (38) make it clear that the millwheel is an emblem of Yvonne's Northern Paradise, her "Columbian Eden" (Cross). The most remarkable passage within the millwheel node comes near the end of chapter 11, when Yvonne experiences a celestial vision that begins vertiginously and ends entropically with her death and the ascension of her soul:

> They were the cars at the fair that were whirling around her; no, they were the planets, while the sun stood, burning and spinning and glittering in the centre; here they came again, Mercury, Venus, Earth, Mars, Jupiter, Saturn, Uranus, Neptune, Pluto; but they were not planets, for it was not a merry-go-round at all, but the Ferris Wheel, they were constellations, in the hub of which, like a great cold eye, burned Polaris, and round and round it here they went: Cassiopeia, Cepheus, the Lynx, Ursa Major, Ursa Minor, and the Dragon; yet they were not constellations, but, somehow, myriads of beautiful butterflies, she was sailing into Acapulco harbour through a hurricane of beautiful butterflies, zigzagging overhead and endlessly vanishing astern over the sea. . . .
> Yvonne felt herself suddenly gathered upwards and borne towards the stars, through eddies of stars scattering aloft with ever wider circling like rings on water, among which now appeared, like a flock of diamond birds flying softly and steadily towards Orion, the Pleiades. . . . (335–36)

Yvonne's death is suggested by the dizzying whirling of the heavens outward and upward in an ever enlarging and continually slowing spiral that disperses into the universe. The millwheel offers a simultaneous but inverted parallel to the developing inferno motif, for if Quauhnahuac is hell in the Consul's mind, it is also just as clearly an "Earthly Paradise" (10), a southern inversion of the Columbian Eden of the north. The luminous wheel thus expresses the constructive and destructive episteme of the work; as Lowry writes, Quauhnahuac "is paradisal: it is unquestionably infernal" (*Letters* 67).

This *discordia concors,* the juxtaposition of demonic and beatific aspects of the wheel, is apparent throughout the novel in clusters of often discordant images, motifs, and recurring details that are placed in proximity to provide thematic development, dramatic tension, and baroque texture and structure. A good example is in chapter 8 where the Consul, Hugh, and Yvonne are riding the bus to Tomalín: "They were crossing a bridge at the bottom of the hill, over the ravine. It appeared overtly horrendous here. . . . Hugh saw a dead dog right at the bottom, nuzzling the refuse; white bones showed through the carcass. But above was the blue sky and Yvonne looked happy when Popocatepetl sprang into view, dominating the landscape for a while as they climbed the . . . long circuitous hill" (233). Within the course of a very few lines, Lowry deploys the motifs of the ravine, the pariah dog, and the inferno, suggested by the hill which eventually "circle[s] down into Tomalín." Yet these demonic motifs are offset by the circular ascent of the characters, the Indian myth of the volcanos as lovers, and the image of blue sky—all of which are associated with the beatific forces of the novel. The paradoxical juxtaposition of motifs reveals Lowry's Manichean episteme, his vision of a black Eden that is a medley of the paradisical and the infernal.

In addition to these nodal clusters that develop the symbolist texture and themes of the novel, there are also numerous nodal signifiers, or simple details that echo major themes and symbols, that while unrelated to the major themes in meaning, are clearly meant to recall them to the reader's mind.[8] A list of such minor nodal signifiers might include the "spinning flywheel of the presses" (54), Hugh standing at the wheel of an imaginary ship (103), the Consul's description of his shakes as "wheels within wheels" (174), his "great wheeling thoughts" (200), the madman with his bicycle tire (224), the bull circling in the arena (257), and the "turning wrenched wheel of a boy's bicycle" (280). Given there are easily over a score of such nodal signifiers, the effect is at once productive of order and disorientation. The desultory surfacing of these signifiers contributes to the structure of disorientation in the work, a structure perfectly suited to a work whose epistemology is simultaneously constructive and destructive.

Conclusion:
Eccentricity and the Horizon of Expectations

Nothing odd will do long.
   —Dr. Johnson to Boswell on *Tristram Shandy*

The most informed of critics seem, in some instances, the least prepared to judge the value of "odd" works. Even though Dr. Johnson is justly regarded as the most knowledgeable and articulate of eighteenth-century critics, he was dead wrong about *Tristram Shandy,* for his strong sense of literary canon and his neoclassical distaste for eccentricity blinded him to the value of Sterne's work. Taste or distaste for a work of literature is, of course, largely dependent on the tension between personal and cultural values, but, as an adherent to and preserver of cultural heritage, Dr. Johnson felt little of this tension and rejected what he probably considered a deformed and grotesque offspring of the novel, itself a bastard form to his mind. We can blink at Johnson's conservative literary politics, living as we do in an iconoclastic age, but we should not dismiss his example, for to do so is to condescend and feel self-important about our own place in literary history; rather, we should take his example as an interesting entrance into the current reevaluation of canon and canonicity.

Most of the heretical texts that have been studied in this book are now part of the established literary canon, and they also constitute a recognizable tradition of their own, distinct from those works of literature that reflect the Christian mythos of the cultural episteme. As such, they are original and eccentric works which, in their time, presented the reader with a defamiliarized vision of the world that was anything but easy to accept. They challenged what Jauss has called the "horizon of expectations" that a reader brings to an initial encounter with a literary text. Seeming either incomprehensible, indecorous, immoral, or all three, these texts disjoin the epistemological codes of culture on linguistic, imagistic, and archetypal levels. But their assimilation into a traditional canon—the way in which they become intelligible and aesthetically valued—is a process as various as the expectations readers bring to the texts.

The idea of canon and its relation to cultural value can be understood by examining the representative responses of selected, well-informed readers (distinct from a more general reading public), who embraced or rejected the eccentric texts in this study on the basis of iconoclastic or cultural values. Although such a selective examination cannot provide a definitive pattern of response, it can suggest how we canonize literature, why some texts become central while others remain eccentric, and why some heretical texts remain eccentric within the heretical tradition they help to form.

The most typical response to an eccentric text is the kind of baffled outrage expressed in Charles Burney's review of Coleridge's "Ancient Mariner":

> The author's first piece, the "Rime of the ancyent Marinere," in imitation of the style as well as the spirit of the elder poets, is the strangest story of a cock and a bull that were ever saw on paper: . . . a rhapsody of unintelligible wildness and incoherence. (Lipking 614)

Burney's observations in the *Monthly Review* (June 1799) reflect his unquestioned adherence to cultural values. His only praise is the implied compliment that Coleridge attempts to imitate the style and spirit of the ancient poets. After this concession, Burney's comments reveal his distaste for the "unintelligible wildness and incoherence" of Coleridge's poem. Such an assessment is ironically appropriate, for Coleridge's poem is meant to be a journey into a supernatural landscape that, foreign to the cultural eye, must be incomprehensible. Coleridge's poetic landscape, which lies beyond the shadow-line, is also beyond the horizon of Burney's expectations. His criticism of

"The Ancient Mariner" is similar to Johnson's assessment of Sterne's novel. Valuing only that which reinforces cultural taste, he is impatient with the eccentricity of the work and cannot appreciate its originality.

The practicing artist, on the other hand, unlike the critic, may have a broader horizon of expectations, a taste for more exotic works. Poe, for example, embraced in De Quincey's *Confessions* the very qualities which Burney objected to in Coleridge. The iconoclastic Poe praises De Quincey's "glorious imagination—deep philosophy—acute speculation" and admires his style which displays "plenty of fire and fury, and a good spicing of the decidedly unintelligible." Poe's savoring of the unintelligible suggests not only that he favors the eccentric but that he finds palatable what De Quincey calls the "literature of Power." Distinguished from the "literature of Knowledge," which engages the reader in discursive thought, the literature of Power offers the reader a blissful escape from the confines of the cultural episteme. While De Quincey admits that most literature is really a blend of the two, a fabric of knowledge and power (Proctor 115), the rare literary work of power—the *Confessions*, for example—appeals to human passions through a blend of imagination, philosophy, fury, and the unintelligible. Despite the eccentricity and, at times, the incomprehensibility of De Quincey's work, Poe's attraction to it is not surprising; what is surprising is that De Quincey's work was so enthusiastically received by a reading public used to literary works of the ordinary blend. The reason for the public's tolerance of eccentricity in De Quincey's first major work may lie in its title. The implication that the *Confessions* was a sort of public act of penance for immoral or socially incomprehensible behavior allowed readers of De Quincey's work to feel morally superior to the author. In the eyes of the contemporary reading public, De Quincey was a repentant, and thus acceptable, eccentric.

It would be a mistake, however, to assume that Poe's taste for De Quincey's "spicing of the decidedly unintelligible" was due simply to his sensibility as an artist, who by temperament is supposedly more capable of embracing the unusual than is the lay public. Many writers, even experimental and highly regarded ones, often find eccentricity strangely unpalatable. A well-known example is Woolf's response to *Ulysses*, a response in keeping with the general English and American view of the work as obscene. Though Woolf, in her essay on "Modern Fiction," praises Joyce's spirituality in *Portrait*, her assessment of *Ulysses* is more ambivalent. In private, she is said to have complained that the book was "underbred" (Ellmann 528), and in a public lecture to the Heretics at Cambridge (a lecture that would become her essay "Mr. Bennet and Mrs. Brown"), Woolf lamented that the experimental writers of her day had "no code of manners" that would serve, in fiction and in life, as a structure of social grace. Such experimental writers, she argued, violate grammar and disintegrate syntax. In particular, she criticized Joyce, saying he did not know when to use a fork or his fingers. Continuing her criticism of Joyce's literary manners, she charged

> Mr. Joyce's indecency in *Ulysses* seems to me the conscious and calculated indecency of a desperate man who feels that in order to breathe he must break the windows. At moments, when the window is broken, he is magnificent. But what a waste of energy! (1:334)

It is tempting, perhaps, to dismiss Woolf's criticism as a kind of rationalized jealousy. And yet the conflict of sensibility is real. Admiring Joyce, Woolf nonetheless finds his work distasteful when he violates the decorum that is the hallmark of her mature style. Woolf's concession that Joyce's iconoclasm is magnificent is a significant one, for it is strikingly similar to Burney's admission that Coleridge's "Ancient Mariner" is rhapsodic even if it is unintelligible. In admitting the power of texts they find distasteful, Burney and Woolf suggest that these eccentric works are, in Barthes's terminology, texts of bliss which undercut the reader's assumptions about social and literary conventions. While experiencing the blissful quality of the text, neither Burney nor Woolf wishes to embrace a work whose literary manners are all wrong.

Woolf felt no such aversion to the dignified prose of Joseph Conrad. In her essay on Conrad, she praises Conrad's "perfect manners" in life and "his beauty" (1:302) as an artist. His fiction, she writes, tells "us something very old and perfectly true; [something] very chaste and very beautiful" (1:308). Though during his lifetime Conrad was not a truly popular writer, in comparison with other writers in this study, he quickly became central to the literary tradition; and, though his reputation has suffered some periods of decline, he has remained part of the canon. His relative popularity might be attributed to the fact that his portrayals of heretical characters who stray from their homeland and cultural values emphasize the danger of such ventures. Conrad's fascination with the incomprehensible ironically culminates in a rejection of the eccentricity and estrangement of so many of his heroes. If Conrad appeals to a broader reading public than Joyce, for instance, this may be because his novels offer a more satisfying, if reductive, resolution of the complex questions of psychology and human perception that they raise. When a cultural heretic like Kurtz dies, the culture itself, at least according to a simplistic reading, is vindicated.

In this sense, individual responses to a work of art can be based on a kind of patriotic aesthetic that confirms a national literature or literary figure. The reception of a work in England and America, for instance, is often different, with critics on one side of the Atlantic singing in unison the praises of a work that is universally condemned on the other side. Barnes's first attempts to have *Nightwood* published in America were met with unanimous resistance. Her biographer notes that *Nightwood* "did not even suffer the usual agonizing delays but shot in and out of publishers' offices as though it were being ejected from a greased revolving door" (Field 207). And after its publication American reviewers attacked the novel as being incomprehensible and even morally reprehensible. Writing in *New Masses*, Philip Rahv titled his review of *Nightwood* "The Taste of Nothing" and described the novel as a "trickle of literarious despair" and "a minute shudder of decadence." He concluded the review lamenting that Barnes's visions of "social decay and sexual perversion have destroyed all response to genuine values and actual things" (34). The novel's reception in England, however, was almost uniformly positive. Edwin Muir, in *The Listener,* praised the "strangeness and the extraordinary verbal beauty of this book. The story itself is simple and comprehensible enough, and is concerned chiefly with the relations between two women" (832). Peter Quennell of *The New Statesman and Nation* praised the "wealth of grotesque and lively imagery" and asserted that "*Nightwood* is not only a strangely original, but . . . an extremely moral work." Quennell continues that he is "not surprised to learn that it appears under the aegis of the most eminent Anglo-Catholic poet of the present day" (592). One wonders to what extent Quennell's admiration and the American distaste for *Nightwood* were influenced by Eliot's favorable introduction to the novel, since his approbation may have suggested to some the book's worthiness for inclusion in the canon. Since there was a good deal of criticism in America of Eliot's introduction—Rahv called *Nightwood* "all T. S. Eliot poetry translated into prose" (33)—the initial American distaste for Barnes may have been more political than aesthetic, since both Barnes and Eliot were estranged from their native land.

Putting aside issues of national taste, the question remains why *Nightwood,* unlike the other eccentric texts examined here, has remained an outsider. The answer may be found by comparing Barnes's work with the work of Malcolm Lowry and considering the intended audiences of their works. If, as Jauss argues, "there are works which at the moment of their publication are not directed at any specific audience, but which break through the familiar horizon of literary expectations so completely that an audience can only gradually develop for them" (16), then the long-standing eccentricity of *Nightwood* and *Under the Volcano* may be understood as a problem of timeliness. Both novels have been recognized as masterful works of genius and yet have remained outside the canon of modern fiction because their most sympathetic readers belong to groups that have tended to lie outside the mainstream of society: lesbians and transsexuals in the case of *Nightwood,* and alcoholics in the case of *Under the Volcano.* While these works are regularly read and appreciated by other reading audiences, each is often said to be too special a case for inclusion in the literary canon. In addition to the "special" subject matter of both books, another reason for their long-term marginality may be that both Barnes and Lowry are often considered one-book authors. A writer with one masterpiece and a series of less perfect works is frequently perceived by the professional reader of literature as having an artistic base too narrow to warrant sustained critical study.

If this book has an implicit critical agenda, it is to question notions of canonicity: to place "central" and "eccentric" works side by side to show that canonized works may themselves be eccentric in their origins and part of a heretical tradition; and, to show that the heretical tradition has its own "central" works, works like Barnes's *Nightwood* and Lowry's *Under the Volcano.* These works, however, which are initially rejected as too eccentric may actually be in the first stage of entering the canon. As Jauss argues, "If the artistic character of a work is to be measured by the aesthetic distance with which it confronts the expectations of its first readers, it follows that this distance, which at first is experienced as a happy or distasteful new perspective, can disappear for later readers" (15). In this way, the work becomes part of and contributes to the culture's expanding horizon of expectations. When an individual reader moves, with a poet or novelist, beyond what the reader has formerly seen only as the horizon, he or she has effectively crossed a personal shadow-line and entered a realm of knowledge previously unimaginable. When many readers move beyond these shadow-lines, cultural belief itself is changed and new shadow-lines, continually moving out to mark the boundary of the known, appear on an ever-expanding horizon.

Notes

Introduction

1. In his preface to *The Order of Things*, Foucault suggests the episteme of a culture is expressed in "the fundamental codes of a culture—those governing its language, its schemas of perception, its exchanges, its techniques, its values, the hierarchy of its practices—[which] establish for every man, from the very first, the empirical orders with which he will be dealing and within which he will be at home" (xx).

2. Ernest Tuveson, In *The Imagination as a Means of Grace: Locke and the Aesthetics of Romanticism* (5–41, esp. 14–15), discusses the "new epistemology" of the materialist tradition in its relation to the English empiricists and romantic poets.

3. Arguing that Locke is a "covert Platonist," A. D. Nuttall in *A Common Sky: Philosophy and the Literary Imagination* suggests that the English empiricists are really hostile to experience as a mode of knowledge (13–23) and thus are part of the idealist philosophy they ostensibly reject.

4. Basil Willey has discussed the influence of the English empiricists on Wordsworth and Coleridge in *The Eighteenth Century Background* (296–309) and traced Coleridge's rejection of Locke and Hartley's materialism in *Nineteenth Century Studies* (13–15). Ernest Tuveson (*The Imagination as a Means of Grace*) outlines the effect of post-Cartesian philosophy on eighteenth- and nineteenth-century theorists of the literary imagination. In *William Wordsworth: His Doctrine and Art in Their Historical Context,* Arthur Beatty traces Wordsworth's connection with Hartley, Godwin, and other British empiricists (97–127). James Engell (*The Creative Imagination: Enlightenment to Romanticism*) places empiricism in a broader, European context and suggests how the romantic theory of the imagination is really a product of the eighteenth century. See also "Wordsworth and the Eighteenth Century" in M. H. Abrams's *The Mirror and the Lamp* (100–114). Most recently, Michael Kearns's *Metaphors of Mind* discusses the relationship of empiricism to metaphors of mind in literature and psychology. Kearns focuses his study on how the metaphorical conception of mind in nineteenth-century England shifted from "mind-as-entity" to "sentience-as-life."

5. Foucault suggests that the classical episteme was based on elements of "resemblance" or "similitude" like the mimetic poesis of Aristotle. That concept of order, Foucault argues, disappeared in the sixteenth and seventeenth centuries and was replaced by the ordering concept of "difference" (46–77) which defines reality not through ordered resemblance but rather through dissociation.

6. For the standard discussions, see Robert Langbaum's introduction to *The Poetry of Experience,* especially 24–28, and M. H. Abrams's *The Mirror and the Lamp.*

7. The relationship between Wittgenstein and the philosophical movement of logical positivism is discussed in Justus Hartnack's *Wittgenstein and Modern Philosophy* (36–48).

8. In *The Milk of Paradise,* M. H. Abrams suggests that opium "may intensify or distort sense perception, especially audition and the visual apprehension of space, structure, light and color" (ix). Clinical studies such as *The Opium Problem* (Terry and Pellens 1928) suggest that the physiological and hallucinogenic effects of opium vary among individuals.

9. Aristotle argues in *De Sensu* that synesthesia is impossible because physiological perception is in essence a sensation within the context of time. He admits to the possibility of fused sensations, but no genuine synesthesia takes place "for the fusion will form a unity and a single sense can perceive a single thing and the single sensation is a chronological unit" (187). He concludes that "when the sensations are not fused, they are two," thereby precluding the possibility of simultaneous perception. Augustine echoes this attitude, suggesting "we can not perceive colors by hearing nor voices by sight" (72). It is not until Locke that synesthesia becomes an accepted mode of perception. Arguing that we have simple and complex ideas, Locke asserts that a kind of synesthesia occurs (Ayer 47) when we apprehend compound sensations from a single object (e.g., ice is sensed as both cold and hard).

One

1. Coleridge's heretical poesy can be distinguished from matters of personal faith. The question of Coleridge's religious development, or rather his vacillation between religious orthodoxy, skepticism, and Unitarianism, has been explored in Barth's *Coleridge and Christian Doctrine* (1969). Abrams (*Natural Supernaturalism* 67) suggests that "Coleridge, who from the time of his maturity was a professing Chris-

tian, carried on a lifetime's struggle to save what seemed to him the irreducible minimum of the Christian creed within an essentially secular metaphysical system." The heresy of Coleridge's poesy exists in his celebration of the human imagination, imagery, and symbolism which explore states of mind that depart from the Christian episteme.

2. Concerning Coleridge as a symbolist, Abrams (*Natural Supernaturalism* 272) quickly dismisses any possibility of "The Ancient Mariner" being a symbolist poem, in part because of the explicitly Christian theme of the poem, but others, such as Daniel Schneider, have suggested that Coleridge is among the first in the symbolist tradition.

3. Abrams, in *The Mirror and the Lamp*, has noted Coleridge's desire to create " 'an involution of the universal in the individual'; the imagination acts by reconciling the opposites of 'the general, with the concrete . . . the individual, with the representative; the sense of novelty and freshness, with old and familiar objects'; and, he says, 'that just proportion, that union and interpenetration of the universal and the particular' " (56). This statement, from the *Biographia Literaria*, suggests the importance of the individual, symbol-making mind.

4. See "The Coalescence of Subject and Object" in I. A. Richards's *Coleridge on Imagination* (44–71).

5. Blake is a mental traveler throughout his career; Byron's central figures, Childe Harold and Juan, make pilgrimages; Shelley's Alastor, Keats's Endymion, and Coleridge's Mariner are all questers.

6. Mircea Eliade in *The Sacred and the Profane* contrasts the concepts of sacred space (within the temple) and profane space (outside of the temple).

7. For the usual (and opposite) archetypal significance of the refusal of return, see Campbell (1949, 193ff.).

8. For the classic treatment of the archetypal significance of descent and cessation of movement, see Maud Bodkin's chapter on "The Ancient Mariner" in *Archetypal Patterns in Poetry;* Frye offers a more recent examination of similar structuralist theories in *The Secular Scripture*.

9. Both Lowes (414ff.) and Daniel Schneider (62) hesitate to identify precisely when Coleridge came under the heavy use of opium. Hayter, however, is more specific, suggesting that Coleridge had used opium during at least four periods between 1791 and the writing of "The Ancient Mariner" (191) and that some of those periods were for

several weeks. All three writers agree that Coleridge was not addicted to opium at the time he wrote "The Ancient Mariner."

10. Abrams (*Natural Supernaturalism* 416–18) mentions Coleridge, De Quincey, and Rimbaud as examples of the modern Christian heretic and makes specific reference to their "heretical" use of drugs to distort the senses.

11. Jasper has suggested that "The Ancient Mariner" contains a duality based on a tension between "the two ontological bases of its form, the one resting upon an ultimate transcendent directing human life and society and the other concealing behind religious platitudes a belief in the self-supporting and sufficient nature of society and the individuals who compose it" (53).

Two

1. For the first substantial examination of De Quincey and the loss of faith, see the chapter on De Quincey in J. Hillis Miller's *The Disappearance of God*.

2. See n. 3, ch. 1.

3. For a discussion of the pictorial qualities of De Quincey's imagination, see Goldman (91).

4. In the revised version of this passage that appears in the "Affliction of Childhood" chapter of the autobiography (46), De Quincey eliminates the phrase "aided by a slight defect in the eyes." It would seem from this that De Quincey himself attached little importance to, or deliberately wished to play down, this physiological aspect of disorientation.

5. These two physiological explanations for De Quincey's "defect" are discussed by Eaton (179–80) and in a letter, 16 August 1809, from De Quincey to Dorothy Wordsworth (Jordan 243–44).

6. De Quincey's various selves and the discrepancy of understanding between them are discussed by Spector (501–20).

7. Referring to De Quincey's digressive wanderings, Miller remarks "to read an essay by De Quincey is to experience a strange and exasperating sense of disorientation, . . . [a] kind of dizzy amazement" (28).

Three

1. Baudelaire's Catholicism is discussed by François Mauriac in "Charles Baudelaire, the Catholic" and Baudelaire's "immanent

Christianity" is explored by Charles Du Bois in "Meditation on the Life of Baudelaire." Both essays are reprinted in *Baudelaire* (Peyre 1962).

2. In his *Confessions,* De Quincey asserts "whereas wine disorders the mental faculties, opium, on the contrary . . . introduces amongst them the most exquisite order, legislation, and harmony. Wine robs a man of his self possession; opium sustains and reinforces it. Wine unsettles the judgment, and gives a preternatural brightness and a vivid exaltation to the contempts and the admirations, to the loves and the hatreds, of the drinker; opium, on the contrary, communicates serenity and equipoise to all the faculties" (3:383).

3. Goldman (1965) defines De Quincey's rifacimento process as a "kind of rewriting, rearranging, and reimagining" (91).

4. Roger Forclaz has argued that through the scientific digressions in *Pym* "Poe separates us from the entire known world by leaving the terrain of scientific exactness in order to give free rein to his imagination. . . . This [documentary] style facilitates the passage from the known to the unknown and renders the transition nearly imperceptible" (46).

5. Detailed analysis of Poe's concern for epistemological questions in "The Fall of the House of Usher" may be found in G. R. Thompson's "Poe and the Paradox of Terror: Structures of Heightened Consciousness in 'The Fall of the House of Usher.'" Thompson's essay, a rebuttal of Partick F. Quinn's "A Misreading of Poe's 'The Fall of the House of Usher,'" is a close textual analysis of references to perception, particularly eyesight, in Poe's tale. Both essays may be found in Thompson and Lokke's *Ruined Eden of the Present.*

Four

1. The question of whether Stephen Dedalus is more influenced by Rimbaud or Baudelaire is addressed by David Weir in "Stephen Dedalus: Rimbaud or Baudelaire?" *JJQ* 18 (1981): 87. These issues are directly addressed by Baudelaire's *Paradis Artificiel* and his 1851 essay "Du Vin et du Hachish" in which he celebrates the *profondes joies du vin.*" Both wine and hashish "*exaltent [la] personnalité,*" but hashish is "*antisocial*" whereas "*la vin est profondément humain.*"

2. In his famous 1871 letter to Izambard, Rimbaud wrote that he was debauching himself as much as possible. He wanted to be poet by making himself a visionary: "*Il s'agit d'arriver a l'inconnu par le dérèglement de tous les sens.*"

3. De Quincey's remark that his poor eyesight aids the visionary sense does not occur in the standard edition of De Quincey's writing (Masson, 1889–90) but in an early version of *Suspiria de Profundis* that first appeared in *Blackwood's* magazine.

4. Eliot's comments on the association of sensibility sound remarkably like a gloss of Stephen's opening lines in "Proteus," which Eliot would have read, in draft form, as early as June 1915 during his stint as assistant editor of *The Egoist* (Ellmann 394; Sultan, 14).

5. For a full discussion of Bloom's androgynous transformations, see Joseph Allen Boone's "A New Approach to Bloom as 'Womanly Man': The Mixed Middling's Progress in *Ulysses*," *JJQ* 20 (1982): 67–86.

6. For the fullest discussion of Joyce's night world in *Finnegans Wake*, see John Bishop's *Joyce's Book of the Dark* (1987).

7. The following summary draws on material from both Tindall and Campbell (1944).

8. Roland McHugh defines sigla as "abbreviations for certain characters or conceptual patterns underlying the book's fabric" (3).

Five

1. J. Hillis Miller (1965) reminds us that "instead of making everything an object for the self, the mind must efface itself before reality, or plunge into the density of an exterior world" (7–8). Similarly, Edward Said stresses that Conrad is interested in presenting the "overriding and immediate sensation of action" (87), and Ian Watt states that Conrad's main objective is "to put us in intense sensory contact with events" (175).

2. Many able critics, following Ford Maddox Ford's lead, have labeled Conrad "a writer who avowed himself impressionist" (Ford vi), but Conrad did not want to be known as "*only* an impressionist" (Garnett 107) and generally used the epithet "impressionistic" unfavorably, at least in a literary context. See Hay, "Joseph Conrad and Impressionism," and Watt, "Impressionism and Symbolism in *Heart of Darkness*," in *Conrad in the Nineteenth Century*.

3. See Adam Gillion, "Conrad as Painter."

4. "Bodies do not produce sensations, but complexes of sensations (complexes of elements) make up bodies. If, to the physicist, bodies appear the real, abiding, existences, whilst sensations are regarded

merely as their evanescent, transitory show, the physicist forgets, in the assumption of such a view, that all bodies are but thought-symbols for complexes of sensations (complexes of elements). Here, too, the *elements* form the real, immediate, and ultimate foundation, which it is the task of physiological research to investigate. . . .

For us, therefore, the world does not consist of mysterious entities, which by their interaction with another, equally mysterious entity, the ego, produce sensations, which alone are accessible. For us, colors, sounds, spaces, times, . . . are all ultimate elements, whose given connexion it is our business to investigate" (Mach 22–23).

5. A similar situation is Brown's meeting with Lord Jim: "A shadow loomed up, moving in the greyness, solitary, very bulky, and yet constantly eluding the eye. . . ." (21:398).

6. See, for instance, Baines (184), Guerard (24, 30, *passim*), Miller (14), and Ian Watt (358).

7. For a discussion of romantic defamiliarization, see Scholes (170–80).

Six

1. References to Lowry's papers, housed in the University of British Columbia's Special Collections, are given by box number, folder, and page reference. They are here quoted and reproduced courtesy of UBC Special Collections and by permission of Literistic Ltd., the literary agent for Lowry's estate. For a bibliography of Lowry's papers, though now somewhat outdated, see Judith O. Combs, *Malcolm Lowry 1909–1957: An Inventory of his Papers in the Library of the University of British Columbia*, Ref. Pub. No. 42 (Vancouver: Univ. of British Columbia Library, 1973).

2. Sherrill Grace in *The Voyage That Never Ends* (1–19) offers a useful synopsis of Lowry's various conceptions of his cycle of novels as well as a detailed summary of how the various works in the cycle are related.

3. Although *Lunar Caustic*, first published by the *Paris Review* and subsequently by Jonathan Cape, is an unrelieved descent into the hellish wards of Bellevue Hospital in New York, Lowry had written several versions of the work, under the various titles of "Lunar Caustic," "The Last Address," and "Swinging the Maelstrom," which present varying degrees of pessimism.

4. For a discussion of Lowry's Eden, see Cross's "Malcolm Lowry and the Columbian Eden."

5. The Consul's mistranslation "You like this garden? Why is it yours? We evict those who destroy!" (128) is corrected later in the novel: "Do you like this garden . . . that is yours? See that your children do not destroy it!" (232). The Consul's misunderstanding at first obscures meaning but also adds an ironic reference to the novel's theme of exile. See Ackerley and Clipper (189–90, 311–12, 446).

6. Ackerley and Clipper discuss the significance of this phrase with regard to the philosophy of *"la vida impersonal"* in which all of humankind is thought to reside in individual Edens, for which each individual is responsible (12, 22–23).

7. Ouspensky discusses Mach's views on sensation in *Tertium Organum* (9, 62–63, 65) and *A New Model of the Universe* (85).

8. The nodes and nodal signifiers that contribute significantly to the fabric of *Volcano* are the luminous wheel, the inferno, Eden, the barranca, horses, the Day of the Dead, Indians and William Blackstone, pariah dogs and Parián, the Farolito, sexual imagery, the Faust legend, the volcanoes, the cinema, the phrase *"no se puede vivir sin amar,"* the movie advertisement *"Las Manos de Orlac.* Con Peter Lorre," the approaching storm, the numbers 666 and 7, birds, insects, and, of course, alcohol and drinking.

Works Cited

Primary Texts

Aquinas, Thomas. *The Basic Writings of Saint Thomas Aquinas.* Ed. Anton C. Pegis. 2 Vols. New York: Random House, 1944.

Aristotle. *Aristotle's Psychology.* Trans. W. A. Hammond. New York: Macmillan, 1902.

Augustine. *The Essential St. Augustine.* New York: New American Library, 1965.

Ayer, A. J., and Raymond Winch, eds. *The British Empirical Philosophers: Locke, Berkeley, Hume, Reid and J. S. Mill.* London: Routledge, 1952.

Barnes, Djuna. "James Joyce." *Vanity Fair* (April 1922): 65.

———. *Nightwood.* New York: New Directions, 1937.

———. "The Call of the Night." *Harper's Weekly* (23 December 1911): 22.

Barthes, Roland. *The Pleasure of the Text.* Trans. Richard Miller. New York: Hill and Wang, 1975.

Baudelaire, Charles. *Œuvres Complètes.* Paris: Aux Editions du Seuil, 1968.

Beach, Sylvia. *Shakespeare & Co.* New York: Harcourt, 1959.

Coleridge, S. T. *Collected Works.* Eds. James Engell and W. Jackson Bate. Bollingen Series, vol. 75. Princeton, N.J.: Princeton Univ. Press, 1983.

Conrad, Joseph. *Complete Works.* 26 vols. New York: Doubleday, 1926.

———. *Conrad's Prefaces to his Works.* Ed. with Intro. by Edward Garnett. London: J. W. Dent, 1937.

Crane, Hart. *Complete Poems and Selected Letters and Prose of Hart Crane.* New York: Doubleday, 1966.

De Quincey, Thomas. *The Collected Writings of Thomas De Quincey.* Ed. David Masson. 14 vols. London: A & C Black, 1896.

Works Cited

———. *A Diary of Thomas De Quincey, 1803.* Ed. Horace A. Eaton. London: Noel Douglas, n.d.

———. *Confessions of an English Opium-Eater and Suspiria de Profundis.* Vol. 1 in *De Quincey's Writings.* 23 vols. Boston: Ticknor, Reed, and Fields, 1951.

Eliot, T. S. *Selected Essays.* New York: Harcourt Brace, 1932.

Foucault, Michel. *The Order of Things.* New York: Random House, 1970.

Gogarty, Oliver St. John. *It Isn't This Time of Year at All.* New York: Doubleday, 1954.

Jauss, Hans Robert. "Literary History as a Challenge to Literary Theory." Trans. Elizabeth Benzinger. *New Literary History* 2 (Autumn 1970): 7–37.

Jolas, Eugene. *The Language of Night.* The Hague: Servivre Press, 1932.

Joyce, James. *Finnegans Wake.* New York: Viking, 1939.

———. *Giacomo Joyce.* New York: Viking, 1968.

———. *Portrait of the Artist as a Young Man.* New York: Viking, 1964.

———. *Stephen Hero.* New York: New Directions, 1944.

———. *Ulysses.* New York: Random House, 1986.

Lawrence, D. H. *Studies in Classic American Literature.* New York: Viking, 1964.

Lowry, Malcolm. *Dark As the Grave Wherein My Friend Is Laid.* New York: New American Library, 1968.

———. *Hear Us O Lord from Heaven Thy Dwelling Place.* Philadelphia: Lippincott, 1961.

———. *Lunar Caustic.* London: Jonathan Cape, 1968.

———. *October Ferry to Gabriola.* New York: World, 1970.

———. *Selected Letters of Malcolm Lowry.* Eds. Harvey Breit and Margerie Lowry. Philadelphia: Lippincott, 1968.

———. *Selected Poems of Malcolm Lowry.* San Francisco: City Lights, 1962.

———. *Ultramarine.* London: Jonathan Cape, 1963.

———. *Under the Volcano*. Philadelphia: Lippincott, 1965.

Lowry Papers. University of British Columbia, Vancouver. Special Collections.

Mach, Ernst. *Contributions to the Analysis of the Sensations*. Chicago: Open Court, 1897.

———. *Knowledge and Error*. Boston: D. Reidel, 1976.

McHugh, Roland. *The Sigla of "Finnegans Wake."* Austin: Univ. of Texas Press, 1976.

Miller, Henry. *The Time of the Assassins*. New York: New Directions, 1946.

Ouspensky, P. D. *A New Model of the Universe*. New York: Random House, 1971.

———. *Tertium Organum*. Rev. ed. Trans. E. Kadloubovsky and P. D. Ouspensky. New York: Random House, 1982.

Plato. *Great Dialogues of Plato*. Trans. W. H. D. Rouse. New York: New American Library, 1956.

Poe, E. A. *The Collected Works of Edgar Allen Poe*. Ed. Thomas Ollive Mabbott. 3 vols. Cambridge, Mass.: Harvard Univ. Press, 1978.

———. *The Narrative of Arthur Gordon Pym of Nantucket*. New York: Penguin, 1975.

Rimbaud, Arthur. *Complete Works, Selected Letters*. Chicago: Univ. of Chicago Press, 1966.

———. *Lettres de la Vie Littéraire d'Arthur Rimbaud*. Paris: Librairie Gallimard, 1931.

Wittgenstein, Ludwig. *The Blue and Brown Books*. New York: Harper, 1958.

———. *Philosophical Investigations*. Trans. G. E. M. Anscombe. Oxford: Basil Blackwell, 1968.

Woolf, Virginia. *Collected Essays*. New York: Harcourt, 1967.

Wordsworth, William. *Literary Criticism of William Wordsworth*. Ed. Paul M. Zall. Lincoln: Univ. of Nebraska Press, 1966.

Secondary Texts

Abrams, M. H. *The Milk of Paradise*. New York: Harper, 1962.

———. *The Mirror and the Lamp*. New York: Oxford Univ. Press, 1953.

———. *Natural Supernaturalism*. London: Oxford Univ. Press, 1971.

Ackerley, Chris, and Lawrence J. Clipper. *A Companion to "Under the Volcano."* Vancouver: Univ. of British Columbia Press, 1984.

Anderson, George K. *The Legend of the Wandering Jew*. Providence, R.I.: Brown Univ. Press, 1965.

Baines, Jocelyn. *Joseph Conrad*. London: Weidenfeld and Nicolson, 1960.

Barth, J. Robert. *Coleridge and Christian Doctrine*. Cambridge, Mass.: Harvard Univ. Press, 1969.

———. "Theological Implications of Coleridge's Theory of Imagination." *Studies in the Literary Imagination* 19 (1986): 23–33.

Beatty, Arthur. *William Wordsworth: His Doctrine and Art in Their Historical Relations*. Madison: Univ. of Wisconsin Press, 1962.

Bersani, Leo. *A Future for Astyanax*. Boston: Little, 1969.

Bishop, John. *Joyce's Book of the Dark*. Madison: Univ. of Wisconsin Press, 1986.

Blackstone, Bernard. *The Lost Travellers*. London: Longmans, 1962.

Blackwood, William. *Joseph Conrad: Letters to William Blackwood and David S. Meldrum*. Durham, N.C.: Duke Univ. Press, 1958.

Blake, Kathleen. "The Whispering Gallery and Structural Coherence in De Quincey's Revised *Confessions of an English Opium-Eater*." *SEL* 13 (1973): 632–42.

Bodkin, Maud. *Archetypal Patterns in Poetry: Psychological Studies of Imagination*. London: Oxford Univ. Press, 1934.

Boone, Joseph Allen. "A New Approach to Bloom as 'Womanly Man': The Mixed Middling's Progress in *Ulysses*." *JJQ* 20 (1982): 67–86.

Bruss, Elizabeth. *Autobiographical Acts*. Baltimore: Johns Hopkins Univ. Press, 1976.

Campbell, Joseph. *The Hero with a Thousand Faces*. Princeton, N.J.: Princeton Univ. Press, 1949.

——— and Henry Morton Robinson. *A Skeleton Key to "Finnegans Wake."* New York: Harcourt Brace, 1944.

Cross, Richard K. *Malcolm Lowry: A Preface to His Fiction.* Chicago: Univ. of Chicago Press, 1980.

———. "Lowry's Columbian Eden." *Contemporary Literature* 14 (1973): 19–30.

Day, Douglas. *Malcolm Lowry.* New York: Oxford Univ. Press, 1973.

De Luca, V. A. *Thomas De Quincey: The Prose of Vision.* Toronto: Univ. of Toronto Press, 1980.

Eaton, Horace Ainsworth. *Thomas De Quincey.* New York: Oxford Univ. Press, 1936.

Eliade, Mircea. *The Sacred and the Profane.* New York: Harcourt, 1957.

Ellmann, Richard. *James Joyce.* New York: Oxford Univ. Press, 1983.

Engell, James. *The Creative Imagination: Enlightenment to Romanticism.* Cambridge, Mass.: Harvard Univ. Press, 1981.

Field, Andrew. *Djuna.* New York: Putnam, 1983.

Forclaz, Roger. "A Voyage to the Frontiers of the Unknown: Edgar Poe's *Narrative of A. Gordon Pym.*" Trans. Gerald Bello. *American Transcendental Quarterly* 37 (1977): 45–56.

Ford, Ford Madox. *Joseph Conrad: A Personal Remembrance.* London: Duckworth & Co., 1924.

Fouchet, Max-Pol. "No Se Puede . . ." *Canadian Literature* 8 (1961): 25–28.

Frye, Northrop. *The Secular Scripture: A Study of the Structure of Romance.* Cambridge, Mass.: Harvard Univ. Press, 1975.

———. *A Study of English Romanticism.* New York: Random House, 1968.

Garnett, Edward, ed. *Letters from Conrad, 1895 to 1924.* London: Nonesuch, 1927.

Gillion, Adam. "Conrad as Painter." *Conradiana* 10 (1978): 53.

Gogarty, Oliver St. John. "They Think They Know Joyce." *Saturday Review of Literature* (18 March 1950): 9.

Goldman, Albert. *The Mind and the Mint.* Carbondale: Southern Illinois Univ. Press, 1965.

Grace, Sherrill. *The Voyage That Never Ends.* Vancouver: Univ. of British Columbia Press, 1982.

Grant, R. M. *Gnosticism and Early Christianity.* New York: Columbia Univ. Press, 1966.

Guerard, Albert J. *Conrad the Novelist.* Cambridge, Mass.: Harvard Univ. Press, 1966.

Hay, Eloise Knapp. "Joseph Conrad and Impressionism." *Journal of Aesthetics and Art Criticism* 34 (1975): 137–44.

Hartnack, Justus. *Wittgenstein and Modern Philosophy.* Trans. Maurice Cranston. London: Methuen, 1962.

Hayman, David. "Nodality and the Infra-Structure of *Finnegans Wake.*" *JJQ* 16 (1977): 135–49.

Hayter, Alethea. *Opium and the Romantic Imagination.* Berkeley: Univ. of California Press, 1970.

Jasper, David. *Coleridge as Poet and Religious Thinker.* Allison Park, Pa.: Pickwick, 1985.

Jean-Aubry, G. *Joseph Conrad: Life and Letters.* 2 Vols. New York: Doubleday, 1927.

Jordan, John E. *De Quincey to Wordsworth.* Berkeley: Univ. of California Press, 1962.

Kannenstine, Louis F. *The Art of Djuna Barnes: Duality and Damnation.* New York: New York Univ. Press, 1977.

Karl, Frederick R. *Joseph Conrad: The Three Lives.* New York: Farrar, Straus & Giroux, 1979.

Kearns, Michael S. *Metaphors of Mind in Fiction and Psychology.* Lexington: Univ. Press of Kentucky, 1987.

Langbaum, Robert. *The Poetry of Experience: The Dramatic Monologue in Modern Literary Tradition.* New York: W. W. Norton, 1957.

Lehmann, A. G. *The Symbolist Aesthetic in France, 1885–1895.* Oxford: Basil Blackwell, 1968.

Lipking, Lawrence. "The Marginal Gloss." *Critical Inquiry* 3 (1977): 609–55.

Lowes, John Livingston. *The Road to Xanadu*. Boston: Houghton, 1927.

Mickel, Emanuel. "Baudelaire's Changing View of the Artificial Paradises." *Romance Notes* 12 (1970): 318–25.

Miller, J. Hillis. *The Disappearance of God: Five Nineteenth-Century Writers*. Cambridge, Mass.: Harvard Univ. Press, 1975.

———. *Poets of Reality: Six Twentieth-Century Writers*. Cambridge, Mass.: Belknap, 1965.

Muir, Edwin. Review of *Nightwood*, by Djuna Barnes. *The Listener* (28 October 1936): 832.

Nuttall, A. D. *A Common Sky: Philosophy and the Literary Imagination*. Berkeley: Univ. of California Press, 1974.

Peckham, Morse. *Victorian Revolutionaries*. New York: George Braziller, 1970.

Peschel, Enid Rhodes. *Flux and Reflux: Ambivalence in the Poems of Arthur Rimbaud*. Geneva: Librairie Droz, 1977.

Peyre, Henri. *Baudelaire*. Englewood Cliffs, N.J.: Prentice-Hall, 1962.

Praz, Mario. *The Romantic Agony*. Trans. Angus Davidson. New York: Meridian, 1956.

Proctor, Sigmund K. *Thomas De Quincey's Theory of Literature*. Ann Arbor: Univ. of Michigan Press, 1943.

Quennel, Peter. Review of *Nightwood*, by Djuna Barnes. *The New Statesman and Nation* (17 October 1936): 592.

Rahv, Philip. Review of *Nightwood*, by Djuna Barnes. *New Masses* (4 May 1937): 32–33.

Richards, I. A. *Coleridge on Imagination*. London: Routledge & Kegan Paul, 1934.

Rickword, Edgell. *Rimbaud: The Boy and the Poet*. Castle Hedlingham, U.K.: Diamon, 1963.

Roppen, Georg, and Richard Sommer. *Strangers and Pilgrims*. Oslo: Norwegian Univ. Press, 1964.

Rosenfield, Claire. *Paradise of Snakes*. Chicago: Univ. of Chicago Press, 1967.

Said, Edward. *Joseph Conrad and the Fiction of Autobiography.* Cambridge, Mass.: Harvard Univ. Press, 1966.

Salveson, Christopher. *The Landscape of Memory.* Lincoln: Univ. of Nebraska Press, 1965.

Schneider, Daniel J. *Symbolism: The Manichean Vision.* Lincoln: Univ. of Nebraska Press, 1975.

Schneider, Elisabeth. *Opium, Coleridge, and "Kubla Khan."* New York: Octagon, 1970.

Scholes, Robert. *Structuralism in Literature.* New Haven, Conn.: Yale Univ. Press, 1974.

Singer, Alan. "The Horse Who Knew Too Much: Metaphor and the Narrative of Discontinuity in *Nightwood.*" *Contemporary Literature* 25 (1984): 66–87.

Spector, Stephen J. "Thomas De Quincey: Self-effacing Autobiographer." *Studies in Romanticism* 18 (1979): 501–20.

Sultan, Stanley. *Ulysses, The Waste Land, and Modernism.* Port Washington, N. Y.: Kennikat Press, 1977.

Tate, Allen. "The Angelic Imagination." In *The Recognition of Edgar Allen Poe,* Ed. Eric W. Carlson. 236–54. Ann Arbor: Univ. of Michigan Press, 1966.

Terry, Charles E., and Mildred Pellens. *The Opium Problem.* New York: Committee on Drug Addictions in collaboration with Bureau of Social Hygiene, 1928.

Thompson, G. R., and Virgil L. Lokke. *Ruined Eden of the Present.* West Lafayette, Ind.: Purdue Univ. Press, 1981.

Tindall, William York. *A Reader's Guide to Finnegans Wake.* New York: Farrar, Straus, & Giroux, 1969.

Tuveson, Ernest. *The Imagination as a Means of Grace: Locke and the Aesthetics of Romanticism.* Berkeley: Univ. of California Press, 1960.

Watt, Cedric. *The Deceptive Text: An Introduction to Covert Plots.* Totowa, N.J.: Barnes, 1984.

Watt, Ian. *Conrad in the Nineteenth Century.* Berkeley: Univ. of California Press, 1979.

Weir, David. "Stephen Dedalus: Rimbaud or Baudelaire?" *JJQ* (18): 87.

Weisstein, Ulrich. "Beast, Doll, and Woman: Djuna Barnes' Human Bestiary." *Renascence* 15 (1962): 3–11.

Wilbur, Richard. "The House of Poe." In *The Recognition of Edgar Allen Poe*, Ed. Eric W. Carlson. 255–77. Ann Arbor: Univ. of Michigan Press, 1966.

Willey, Basil. *The Eighteenth Century Background*. New York: Columbia Univ. Press, 1950.

———. *Nineteenth Century Studies*. New York: Columbia Univ. Press, 1949.

Index

Abrams, M. H., 14, 16
Aeneid, 17, 43
Aiken, Conrad, 125
Animism, 20, 25, 59, 108, 127–28, 131; beatific, 128–30; demonic, 128–30
Archetypes:
—of death and rebirth, 17, 18, 22, 52–56, 106
—of the fall, 1, 16, 33, 74
—of heaven and hell, 30, 115, 137–39
—subversion of, 13–14, 30–33, 54–55, 74, 114. *See also* Disorientation, archetypal
Aristotle, 3–5, 7, 68, 71, 90
Augustine, St., 4

Barnes, Djuna, 9, 12, 65–66, 73, 76–85, 144–45; and James Joyce, 65–66, 76. Works: "Call of the Night," 77; "James Joyce," 65; *Nightwood,* 66, 76–84, 86, 144–46
Barthes, Roland, 10, 71
Baudelaire, Charles, 12, 45–52, 55, 60, 64, 85, 100; and *Club des hachischins,* 48; and De Quincey, 45–48; and theory of *correspondances,* 49–50. Works: "Correspondances," 49–50; "Du vin et du hachish," 46, 60; "L'Invitation au Voyage," 50–51; "Le Poëme du Haschisch," 47–48, 60; "Le Voyage," 51; *Un Mangeur Opium,* 47–48
Beach, Sylvia, 65
Berkeley, George, 6–7, 71

165

Birney, Earl, 123
Blackstone, Bernard, 16
Blake, William, 83
Bodkin, Maud, 18, 21
Boehme, Jakob, 71
Borda, José de la, 132
Boswell, James, 15, 27
Burney, Charles, 141–43

Canon, the literary, 140–41, 145–46
Cape, Jonathan, 116, 132, 136
Coleridge, Samuel Taylor, 9, 12–25, 35, 50, 53, 63, 87, 100, 113; and the subversion of archetypes, 17–27; and the symbolist imagination, 13–15; and the Wordsworthian journey, 15–17. Works: *Biographia Literaria,* 13, 23; "The Rime of the Ancient Mariner," 17–25, 28–29, 54, 56–57, 66, 73, 75, 105, 122, 131, 141, 143
Conrad, Joseph, 1–2, 8–9, 12, 81, 85–114, 125, 144; decoding, 95; impressionism of, 92; treatment of knowledge, 91–99; treatment of sensation, 91–99; treatment of visionary moment (image), 99–103. Works: "Heart of Darkness," 87, 95, 103, 106–7, 111; *Lord Jim,* 93–94, 100–1; *The Mirror of the Sea,* 85; *The Nigger of the "Narcissus,"* 102, 107; preface to *The Nigger of the "Narcissus,"* 89, 109; *Nostromo,* 94–97, 101, 106, 111; "An Outpost of Progress," 91–93, 96, 101–2, 109–10, 112–13; *The Secret Agent,* 86; "The Secret Sharer," 112; *The Shadow-Line,* 1, 104–6; *Typhoon,* 97–99, 107–8, 110; *Victory,* 110
Crane, Hart, 61

Dana, Richard H., 125
Dante Alighieri, 116
Defoe, Daniel, 15
Demeny, Paul, 60
De Quincey, Thomas, 9, 12, 26–44, 45–46, 50, 52–53, 57, 60, 63–64, 69, 85, 87, 99, 100, 120; on analogues of opium intoxication, 33–44; on dreaming and opium visions, 30–33; and Wordsworthian tradition, 27–30. Works: *Autobiography,* 35, 37; *Confessions of an English Opium-Eater,* 26–33, 39, 43–45, 47–48, 105, 142; *Diary,* 38; *The English Mail-Coach,* 26, 41–2; *Suspiria de Profundis,* 26, 33–34, 38–40, 69
Descartes, René, 5
Dickinson, Emily, 45
Disorientation, literary tradition of, 12
—archetypal: 10–12. See also Archetypes, subversion of

—imagistic/symbolic: 10–12, 22, 38, 123–32; through iconoclasm, 11, 21. *See also* Disorientation, sensory
—linguistic: 10–11, 22–23, 42–43, 55, 65, 70–71, 80–84, 118–22; through competing texts, 22–23, 75–76, 82–83, 122; through digression, 42–43, 57; through disintegration of language, 72; through mistranslation, 121; through multilingual puns or malapropisms, 74, 118, 120–22; through neologisms, 72
—sensory: 9–12, 17, 25, 36, 38, 43, 64–72, 74, 76–78, 84, 87, 94, 103–4, 107, 110, 125, 133; through anesthesia, 11, 87, 105–7, 113; through *dérèglement de tous les sens*, 39, 60–61, 64, 67–68, 133; through entropy, 52, 123, 125, 127, 132–35; through hyperesthesia, 11, 20, 22, 28–29, 34–36, 40–43, 48, 52–53, 55, 59, 97, 113; through synesthesia, 11, 20, 22, 29, 41–42, 48, 52–53, 63, 87, 97, 107; through vertigo, 44, 52–53, 63, 105, 111, 120–21, 123, 125–27, 132–33, 135, 137
Donne, John, 68
Dreams, 34, 40, 42, 48, 78, 84, 111–12; opium, 50, 106

Eccentricity, 140–42, 146
Eliot, T. S., 68, 145
Episteme:
—Christian, cultural: 2, 6, 9–10, 14–15, 18, 30, 32, 53–54, 64, 84, 87, 114, 140, 142; disjoining or subversion of, 9, 11–12, 15, 21, 25, 30, 50, 58–59, 63, 66, 69–70, 76, 84, 86, 110, 113, 127, 141; estrangement from its values, 2, 10, 12, 17, 47, 51, 55, 61–65, 70, 74, 76–78, 104, 109, (through cannibalism) 56–57, 86, (through intoxication) 61, (through sexual practices) 65, 73, 79–81; values of, 57, 68, 70, 73, 82, 140–41
—heretical: 2, 14; and Manichean world view, 115, 117, 127, 132, 139; and the mythopoeic imagination, 7, 14, 21, 30
Epistemology(ies): competing, 117; constructive/destructive, 63, 117–18, 120–21, 125–26, 128, 130–31, 137–39; sensationalist, 89; schizophrenic, 115, 118

Foucault, Michel, 2
Fouchet, Max-Pol, 133
Frye, Northrop, 14, 16

Garnett, Edward, 87–88
Gogarty, Oliver St. John, 67
Gosse, Edmund, 85
Grace, Sherrill, 117
Grieg, Nordahl, 125

Hayman, David, 135–36
Horizon of expectations, 140–41, 145–46
Hume, David, 6

Intoxication, imagery of, 9, 52, 66–67, 122, 125
—alcohol-induced, 9, 31, 46, 60, 132–33
—hashish-induced, 48
—opium-induced, 9, 20, 27, 30–31, 34, 38, 40–41, 46–48, 55, 58, 105, 113. *See also* Disorientation, sensory
Isambard, Georges, 60

Jauss, Hans Robert, 140, 145–46
Johnson, Samuel, 15, 27, 140, 142
Jolas, Eugene, 8, 65, 72
Journey, 12, 15, 27
—circular (Christian), 12, 16, 22, 24, 52–53, 114, 116
—disorienting: 16–18, 20, 25–26, 64, 85–87, 103, 105–14; across the shadow-line, 1–2, 12, 14–15, 19, 22, 28–29, 85, 87, 106–7, 146; of estrangement from homeland, 46, 50, 54, 145, (and theme of the pariah, 26, 109, 137, 139); into heretical space, 12, 17, 20, 27–28, 53–55, 84, 114
—linear, 17, 27, 52, 54–55, 117
Joyce, James, 8–9, 12, 65–76, 81, 84, 100. Nocturnal vision: and association of sensibility, 68; and discontinuous narrative structures, 70–71, 74–76; and epiphany, 66–68; and hallucination, 72–74; and visual disorientation, 69–70. Works: *Finnegans Wake*, 74–76; *Giacomo Joyce*, 70–71; *Portrait of the Artist As a Young Man*, 67–69, 74, 79–80, 118, 143; *Stephen Hero*, 67, 69; *Ulysses*, 65, 70–74, 80, 84, 86, 118, 143

Kannenstine, Louis, 80, 83

Lawrence, D. H., 52
Locke, John, 1, 6
London, Jack, 125
Lowry, Malcolm, 9, 12, 115–39; competing world views, 123–32; cycle of novels, 115–18; structure of *Under the Volcano*, 132–39; treatment of language, 118–22. Works: *Dark As the Grave Wherein My Friend Is Laid*, 116, 118, 132; "The Forest Path to the Spring," 117, 119, 128, 130–31; *Hear Us O Lord From Heaven Thy Dwelling Place*, 122, 128; *In Ballast to the White Sea*, 116; *La Mordida*, 116; *Lunar Caustic*, 116–17, 123, 125–26, 130–31; *October Ferry to Gabriola*, 116, 119, 128; *The Ordeal of Sigbjørn Wilderness 1*, 116; *The Ordeal of Sigbjørn Wilderness 2*, 116–17; "Through the Panama," 122;

Ultramarine, 116, 125–26; *Under the Volcano,* 116–23, 129, 132–39, 145–46; *The Voyage That Never Ends,* 115–117; "Work in Progress," 116; papers of, 115, 123–24
Lowry, Margerie, 119, 123

Mach, Ernst, 7–8, 89–90, 95–96
Mill, John Stewart, 45
Miller, Henry, 65
Models of mind: empiricist, 5, 88; idealist/rationalist, 4, 7; mechanical, 33–44, 105; romantic, 6–7, 13; sensationalist, 89
Muir, Edwin, 145

Newman, Henry, 45
Nicolay, Helen, 122
Nietzsche, Friedrich, 124–25
Nobel, Edward, 90, 100
Nodal structure, 135–39

Odyssey, 17
Ouspensky, P. D., 124–25

Peckham, Morse, 23
Pethick, Derek, 115
Plato, 3–4
Poe, Edgar Allen, 9, 12, 45, 52–60, 64, 85–86, 142; and archetypal journey, 52–53; and cultural value, 55–57; and relation to French symbolists, 52, 64. Works: "A Descent into the Maelström," 52–53, 56, 58; "The Fall of the House of Usher," 58–59; "MS. Found in a Bottle," 52, 54–56, 58; *The Narrative of Arthur Gordon Pym of Nantucket,* 52, 55–58
Praz, Mario, 17
Proust, Marcel, 115–16
Pulman, Adam Marek, 88

Quennell, Peter, 145

Rahv, Philip, 144
Representation, 7, 9, 13
Rimbaud, Arthur, 45, 54–64, 66–67, 69, 72, 87, 127, 133; and Baudelaire, 60; letters of the *voyant,* 60–61. Works: "Le Bateau ivre," 61–63; "Voyelles," 60
Roppen, Georg, and Sommer, 17

Said, Edward, 92
Shakespeare, William, 1
Smollett, Tobias, 15

Sommer, Richard, and Roppen, 17
Spectral persecution, 21, 33, 55
Sterne, Lawrence, 140, 142
Swedenborg, Emanuel, 49
Swift, Jonathan, 15
Symbolism, 20; involute, 35–36, 40, 50; involution, 15, 35, 100. *See also* Disorientation, symbolic
Symbolist tradition, 9, 13–15, 17, 30, 36, 45–52, 59–64, 66, 85

Text of Bliss, 10, 71, 143
Thomas, Aquinas, 4

Visionary experience, types of, 32, 112–13
—*correspondances*, 48–50, 52–53, 60, 100
—dream vision, 66, 74, 113
—epiphany, 66–67, 69, 71, 74, 100
—hallucination, 72–74
—hypnogogic vision, 30, 74, 112, 126
—image, 99–104
—moment, 44, 91, 100, 102–3
—perceptual frame in, 32, 38–39, 40–41, 44, 98–99. *See also* Disorientation, sensory

Watt, Ian, 92
Wittgenstein, Ludwig, 8
Woolf, Virginia, 143–44
Wordsworth, William, 13–14, 28, 31–32, 34, 37, 44; and Christian mythos, 15–17; and Coleridge, 13–15; and De Quincey, 26–28, 44. Works: *Lyrical Ballads,* 13, 15; *Prelude,* 16, 27, 32

PR 888 .A42 C76 1989

Bock, Martin, 1951-

Crossing the shadow-line

DATE DUE